It's another Quality Book from CGP

This book is a guide to all three of our Functional Question books: Higher Level, Foundation Level and Foundation Level — the Basics.

It shows which maths topics are covered by each question, so you can check whether your class has covered those topics before you set work.

It also includes full worked solutions to every question in each of the three books.

What CGP is all about

Our sole aim here at CGP is to produce the highest quality books — carefully written, immaculately presented and dangerously close to being funny.

Then we work our socks off to get them out to you — at the cheapest possible prices.

Contents

Guide to Themes and Topics — Foundation Level — the Basics 1

Answers (Foundation Level — the Basics) 5

Guide to Themes and Topics — Foundation Level 16

Answers (Foundation Level) 20

Guide to Themes and Topics — Higher Level 34

Answers (Higher Level) 38

Published by CGP

Editors:
Katie Braid, Rosie Gillham, David Ryan, Jane Towle, Karen Wells, Dawn Wright.

ISBN: 978 1 84762 519 9

Images of bus and timetable on front cover supplied courtesy of Stagecoach Group.

Height/Weight chart on front cover from The Food Standards Agency © Crown copyright reproduced under the terms of the Click-use Licence.

Groovy website: www.cgpbooks.co.uk

Printed by Elanders Ltd, Newcastle upon Tyne.
Jolly bits of clipart from CORELDRAW®

Based on the classic CGP style created by Richard Parsons.

Photocopying — it's dull, it takes ages... and sometimes it's a bit naughty. Luckily, it's dead cheap, easy and quick to order more copies of this book from CGP — just call us on 0870 750 1242. Phew!
Text, design, layout and original illustrations © Coordination Group Publications Ltd. (CGP) 2010
All rights reserved.

Guide to Themes and Topics
Foundation Level — The Basics

Party 1
    Q1: *Two-way Tables, Financial Arithmetic (Non-Calculator)*
    Q2: *Arithmetic (Non-Calculator), Conversion Factors (Metric)*
    Q3: *Arithmetic, Proportion*
    Q4: *Time*
    Q5: *Two-way Tables*
    Q6: *Conversion Factors (Metric-Imperial), Rounding*
    Q7: *Arithmetic*
    Q8: *Probability*

Holidays 5
    Q1: *Bar-Line Graphs*
    Q2: *Financial Arithmetic*
    Q3: *Two-way Tables, Financial Arithmetic*
    Q4: *Timings and Timetables*
    Q5: *Bar Charts, Line Graphs*
    Q6: *Bar Charts, Financial Arithmetic*
    Q7: *Two-way Tables, Financial Arithmetic*
    Q8: *Timings and Timetables*

Transport 9
    Q1: *Financial Arithmetic*
    Q2: *Financial Arithmetic*
    Q3: *Timings and Timetables*
    Q4: *Maps and Scale Drawings*
    Q5: *Time, Financial Arithmetic*
    Q6: *Maps and Scale Drawings, Conversion Factors (Metric-Imperial)*
    Q7: *Compound Measures (Speed), Time*
    Q8: *Compound Measures (Speed), Time*

Food and Drink 13
    Q1: *Two-way Tables, Time, Fractions*
    Q2: *Time*
    Q3: *Conversion factors (Metric-Imperial), Formulas*
    Q4: *Proportion*
    Q5: *Scales and Measurements, Fractions*
    Q6: *Scales and Measurements*
    Q7: *Proportion*
    Q8: *Ratios*

Guide to Themes and Topics
Foundation Level — The Basics

Day Trip 17
    Q1: *Timings and Timetables*
    Q2: *Financial Arithmetic (Non-Calculator)*
    Q3: *Financial Arithmetic (Non-Calculator)*
    Q4: *Arithmetic (Non-Calculator)*
    Q5: *Time, Financial Arithmetic*
    Q6: *Timings and Timetables*
    Q7: *Financial Arithmetic, Formulas*
    Q8: *Financial Arithmetic, Two-way Tables*

Shopping 21
    Q1: *Fractions*
    Q2: *Financial Arithmetic, Percentages*
    Q3: *Financial Arithmetic*
    Q4: *Percentages, Fractions, Financial Arithmetic*
    Q5: *Financial Arithmetic, Percentages*
    Q6: *Financial Arithmetic, Percentages*
    Q7: *Financial Arithmetic, Fractions*
    Q8: *Best Buys*

Jobs 25
    Q1: *Financial Arithmetic*
    Q2: *Financial Arithmetic*
    Q3: *Proportions*
    Q4: *Financial Arithmetic*
    Q5: *Calculating Averages and Spread*
    Q6: *Percentages*
    Q7: *Calculating Averages and Spread, Financial Arithmetic*
    Q8: *Percentages*

Going Out 29
    Q1: *Time*
    Q2: *Rounding, Financial Arithmetic (Non-Calculator)*
    Q3: *Two-way Tables, Financial Arithmetic (Non-Calculator), Percentages*
    Q4: *Financial Arithmetic (Non-Calculator)*
    Q5: *Timings and Timetables*
    Q6: *Best Buys*
    Q7: *Financial Arithmetic*
    Q8: *Financial Arithmetic, Percentages, Rounding*

Guide to Themes and Topics
Foundation Level — The Basics

Decorating 33
- Q1: *Arithmetic*
- Q2: *Perimeter*
- Q3: *Area, Financial Arithmetic*
- Q4: *Estimating*
- Q5: *Area, Financial Arithmetic*
- Q6: *Tessellation, Area, Rounding*
- Q7: *Ratios*
- Q8: *Calculation Bounds, Rounding*

Gardening 37
- Q1: *Area*
- Q2: *Financial Arithmetic*
- Q3: *Area, Financial Arithmetic*
- Q4: *Perimeter, Financial Arithmetic*
- Q5: *Area, Estimating, Proportion*
- Q6: *Proportion*
- Q7: *Scale Drawings*
- Q8: *Circumference*

City Planning 41
- Q1: *Arithmetic*
- Q2: *Number Sequences*
- Q3: *Bar Charts, Arithmetic*
- Q4: *Percentages, Financial Arithmetic, Large Numbers*
- Q5: *Perimeter, Area*
- Q6: *Projections, Scale Drawings*
- Q7: *Area, Line Graphs*
- Q8: *Pie Charts, Percentages*

Paying Bills 45
- Q1: *Financial Arithmetic*
- Q2: *Financial Arithmetic*
- Q3: *Financial Arithmetic*
- Q4: *Financial Arithmetic, Percentages*
- Q5: *Financial Arithmetic, Percentages*
- Q6: *Two-way Tables, Financial Arithmetic*

Guide to Themes and Topics
Foundation Level — The Basics

In the News **48**
    Q1: *Bar Charts*
    Q2: *Arithmetic, Probability*
    Q3: *Pie Charts, Sampling and Data Collection*
    Q4: *Calculating Averages and Spread*
    Q5: *Sampling and Data Collection*
    Q6: *Pie Charts*

Health and Fitness **51**
    Q1: *Financial Arithmetic*
    Q2: *Tally Charts, Calculating Averages*
    Q3: *Frequency Tables*
    Q4: *Calculating Averages*
    Q5: *Sampling and Data Collection*
    Q6: *Distance-Time Graphs*
    Q7: *Scatter Graphs and Correlation*
    Q8: *Calculating Averages*

Car Boot Sale **55**
    Q1: *Financial Arithmetic (Non-Calculator)*
    Q2: *Financial Arithmetic (Non-Calculator)*
    Q3: *Rounding*
    Q4: *Financial Arithmetic (Non-Calculator)*
    Q5: *Volume of 3D Shapes*
    Q6: *Financial Arithmetic (Non-Calculator)*
    Q7: *Percentages*
    Q8: *Percentages, Financial Arithmetic*

Banking **59**
    Q1: *Financial Arithmetic*
    Q2: *Financial Arithmetic, Percentages*
    Q3: *Fractions, Percentages*
    Q4: *Financial Arithmetic*
    Q5: *Financial Arithmetic, Fractions*
    Q6: *Financial Arithmetic*
    Q7: *Financial Arithmetic, Percentages*
    Q8: *Financial Arithmetic, Percentages, Rounding*

Answers (Foundation Level — The Basics): P.1 — P.7

Party

Page 1
Q1 a) 5 of her guests have special diets.
  b) 5 × £9 = £45.
Q2 a) Each bottle contains 1.5 litres. Jess has bought 3 bottles so has 3 × 1.5 = 4.5 litres.
  b) 1 litre is 1000 ml, so 4.5 litres is 4.5 × 1000 = 4500 ml.
  c) Each cup holds 500 ml so Jess can pour 4500 ÷ 500 = 9 cups.

Page 2
Q3 a) Each person is having 4 slices of pizza so Rupert needs 10 × 4 = 40 slices.
  b) Each pizza has 8 slices so he needs 40 ÷ 8 = 5 pizzas.
  c) Each person is having 25 g of crisps so he needs 25 × 10 = 250 g. Each packet contains 300 g so he needs 1 packet of crisps.
Q4 a) The ham and peanut pizza needs to cook for 10 mins so she should take it out at 10:20 pm. The squirrel pizza needs to cook for 20 mins so she should take it out at 10:30 pm.
  b) The potato pizza can go into the oven at 10:20 pm. It needs to cook for 15 mins so it's due out at 10:35 pm.
  c) The cabbage pizza can go in the oven at 10:30 pm at the earliest. It needs to cook for 15 mins so the earliest time it can be ready is 10:45 pm.

Page 3
Q5 a), b) and c)

	Game 1	Game 2	Game 3	Total
Team 1	5	5	10	20
Team 2	2	10	5	17
Team 3	10	2	2	14

  c) Team 1 won.
Q6 a) Nick: 68 kg is 68 × 2.2 = 150 pounds (to nearest pound). Tim: 88 kg is 88 × 2.2 = 194 pounds (to nearest pound).
  b) Simon: 13 stone is 13 × 14 = 182 pounds. 182 + 8 = 190 pounds. Joe: 10 stone is 10 × 14 = 140 pounds. 140 + 3 = 143 pounds.

Page 4
Q7 a) 32 ÷ 12 = 2.6666... so each bag can have 2 chocolate bars.
  b) 90 ÷ 12 = 7.5, so each bag can have 7 animals.
  c) 90 − 9 = 81. 81 ÷ 12 = 6.75, so each bag can have 6 animals.
Q8 a) There are 12 cakes in total and 4 lemon flavoured ones, so the probability of Ken picking a lemon flavoured cake is $\frac{4}{12} = \frac{1}{3}$.
  b) There are 5 fish sauce flavoured cakes, so the probability of Ken picking a fish sauce flavoured cake is $\frac{5}{12}$.
  The probability of not picking a fish sauce flavoured cake is: $1 - \frac{5}{12} = \frac{12}{12} - \frac{5}{12} = \frac{7}{12}$.

Holidays

Page 5
Q1 a) The highest snowfall is in January.
  b) In October there is an average of 15 cm of snow per day.
Q2 a) Lola will need £245 + £164 + £52.50 + £43.50 = £505.
  b) She will have £600 − £505 = £95 left for spending money.
  c) With an extra £43.50, she will have £95 + £43.50 = £138.50.

Page 6
Q3 a) Need Oak Cabin for 2 nights at £150 per night. Total cost = £150 × 2 = £300.
  b) Each person will owe £300 ÷ 6 = £50.
Q4 a) The latest train to get to Travistown before 9 pm (2100) leaves Wrigly at 1920, or 7.20 pm.
  b) The only train between 5 and 6 pm is the 1735, which gets in at 1903, so Will should ask Mike to meet them at 7.03 pm.
  c) The train leaves Wrigly at 1735, or 5.35 pm. Will needs to set off 15 mins before this, at 5.20 pm. So between 3.30 pm and 5.20 pm he has 1 hour and 50 mins to pack.

Page 7
Q5 a) June, July, August and September.
  b) Of the months with the right temperature, July has the lowest rainfall so they should plan the holiday for July.
Q6 a) The flight out on the 11th costs £35. Fiona will need to return 7 days later on the 18th, which costs £45. Cost of both flights = £35 + £45 = £80.
  b) Total cost = £80 for flights + £15.75 + £11.50 = £107.25.

Answers (Foundation Level — The Basics): P.8 — P.14

Page 8
Q7 a) One week in June half board will cost £270 per adult and £270 ÷ 2 = £135 per child. Total cost for 2 adults and 2 children = (2 × £270) + (2 × £135) = £810.
b) For full board, one week in June will cost: (2 × £300) + (2 × £150) = £900. So they can afford to go full board on a budget of £950.

Q8 a) The family need to arrive at the airport no later than 45 minutes before 1300 = 1215.
b) The latest train they could get which would get them to the airport for 1215 is the 1022 from Chorley. They need to set off 15 mins + 5 mins = 20 mins before this, so the latest time they can leave the house is 1002 (10:02 am).

Transport
Page 9
Q1 a) 30 + 28 + 40 = 98 miles.
b) 22p is given for each mile travelled, so she should get 22 × 98 = 2156p (£21.56).

Q2 a) Outbound flight + inbound flight costs 29.99 + 34.99 = £64.98 per person. For both Mark and Rose to fly it will cost 64.98 × 2 = £129.96.
b) To get the train to London it would cost them £98 each, so 98 × 2 = £196 in total. So it's cheaper for them to fly.

Page 10
Q3 a) He will arrive in Preston at 10.25. The interview is a 15 minute walk away so he will get there at 10.40.
b) Colin catches the 10.08 bus which will get him to Preston at 10.40. The interview is a 15 minute walk from the bus station so he will get there at 10.55. So yes, he will be in time for his interview.

Q4 a) Measure each stage of the journey between Oaks and Furly on the map and add them together:
2 cm + 2 cm + 1.5 cm + 1 cm = 6.5 cm.
1 cm = 4 miles, so 6.5 cm is 6.5 × 4 = 26 miles.
b) Measure the distance between Furly and Cefn:
1 + 1.5 + 1 + 1.5 + 2 = 7 cm.
7 cm is 7 × 4 = 28 miles.

Page 11
Q5 a) If Caroline takes the ferry she will leave at 19:30 and travel for 2 hours 30 mins. So she will get there at 22:00. If she flies she will leave at 19:55 and travel for an hour, so she will get there at 20:55. So the earliest she could arrive would be 20:55.
b) Cost on the ferry is:
£36.90 + £24.30 = £61.20.
Cost on the plane is:
£33.90 + £29.90 = £63.80.
So Caroline should travel by ferry.

Q6 a) Distance on the map from Fleetley to Goole: 2 + 1.5 + 2 = 5.5 cm.
5.5 cm is 5.5 × 5 = 27.5 km.
b) 1 km is 0.6 miles so 27.5 km is 27.5 × 0.6 = 16.5 miles.

Page 12
Q7 a) Phil drives at 50 mph and he has 150 miles to drive.
Time = Distance ÷ Speed
so it will take him:
150 miles ÷ 50 mph = 3 hours.
b) The whole journey will take 3 hours + 30 mins + 30 mins = 4 hours.
c) Phil sets off at 4 pm English time. He drives for 4 hours so arrives at 8 pm English time, which is 9 pm in France.

Q8 a) Jamie's house is 15 miles away. She travels at 30 mph.
Time = Distance ÷ Speed
so it will take her:
15 miles ÷ 30 mph = 0.5 hours.
0.5 hours × 60 = 30 minutes.
b) Brad's house is 10 miles away. She travels at 30 mph.
Time = Distance ÷ Speed
so it will take her:
10 miles ÷ 30 mph
= 0.3333... hours.
0.3333... hours × 60 = 20 mins.
If she leaves at 10 am she will get there at 10.20 am.

Food and Drink
Page 13
Q1 a) 3½ + 1 + 1½ = 6 mins.
b) He needs to start it 6 mins before 7.30 pm = 7.24 pm.

Q2 a) Turkey needs 40 mins per kg × 5 kg = 200 mins = 3 hrs 20 mins.
b) Turkey will take in total 3 hours and 20 mins + 10 mins = 3 hours 30 mins, so she should start it at 10.00 am.
c) Potatoes take 10 mins + 20 mins + 50 mins = 1 hour 20 mins.
d) Chloe needs to start 1 hour 20 mins before 1.30 pm, at 12.10 pm.

Page 14
Q3 a) Using 1 lb ≈ 450 g:
Butter ≈ 1 lb × 450 = 450 g.
Sugar ≈ 1½ lb × 450 = 675 g.
Flour ≈ 2 lb × 450 = 900 g.
b) Using 1 pint ≈ 570 ml.
Milk ≈ ½ pint × 570 ml = 285 ml.
c) °C ≈ (330 °F − 30) ÷ 2 = 150 °C.

Q4 36 cakes ÷ 12 cakes = 3, so Laura needs to divide the amounts of all the ingredients by 3:
Butter: 375 g ÷ 3 = 125 g.
Sugar: 750 g ÷ 3 = 250 g.
Flour: 600 g ÷ 3 = 200 g.
Eggs: 6 eggs ÷ 3 = 2 eggs.
Milk: 360 ml ÷ 3 = 120 ml.

Answers (Foundation Level — The Basics):   P.15 — P.20

Page 15
Q5 a) Each division on the scale is 1 oz. The scale reads 10 oz, but it should read 6½ + 4½ = 11 oz, so he needs to add another ounce of sugar.
b) Flour and sugar = 11 oz, so with butter the weight should be 11 oz + 5½ oz = 16½ oz, or 1 lb and ½ oz.

Q6 a) 170 g lentils needed so use: 100 g + 50 g + 20 g = 170 g.
b) Four carrots weigh 300 g. This is half the amount needed, so Jo needs four more carrots.
c) Each division on the scale is 100 ml ÷ 4 = 25 ml. Jug scale reads 125 ml, so she needs 150 ml − 125 ml = 25 ml more.

Page 16
Q7 a) For 24 people, Jake needs to scale up the recipe for sausage rolls by 2. So he needs 1 onion × 2 = 2 onions.
b) Jake needs 1 egg × 2 = 2 eggs for the sausage rolls. He also needs eggs for the cheesy biscuits. The biscuit recipe needs to be scaled up by 3, so he needs 1 egg × 3 = 3 eggs for the cheesy biscuits. In total he needs 2 + 3 = 5 eggs.
c) For the cheesy biscuits Jake needs 100 g × 3 = 300 g cheese. He needs to buy 300 g − 200 g = 100 g more cheese.

Q8 a) To make 10 litres, Jake needs to scale up the recipe by 10 ÷ 5 = 2.
Orange juice: 2 litres × 2 = 4 litres.
Ginger ale: 3 litres × 2 = 6 litres.
b) Jake needs 3 parts ginger ale for every 2 parts of orange juice. If 2 parts of orange juice = 3 litres, then 1 part = 3 ÷ 2 = 1.5 litres.
So he needs 3 parts × 1.5 litres per part = 4.5 litres of ginger ale.

c) 1 part is 1.5 litres, so Jake needs 1.5 litres of pineapple juice. Using this recipe he will have: 1.5 litres pineapple juice + 3 litres orange juice + 4.5 litres ginger ale = 9 litres of punch.

Day Trip
Page 17
Q1 a) Sea lions, polar bears, meerkats, monkeys, tigers, lions, penguins.
b) Between the feeding times of the monkeys and tigers.

Q2 Total cost of plane museum: 5.20 + 3.90 = £9.10.
Total cost of postal museum: 3.50 + 1.70 = £5.20.
Total cost of police museum: 4.50 + 0.60 = £5.10.
She should go to the police museum.

Page 18
Q3 a) Total cost is: 5 + 15 + 15 + 50 + 50 = £135.
b) Cost of parking and bikes is 15 + 15 + 5 = £35. So Nigel owes Helen £35 ÷ 2 = £17.50.

Q4 a) 9.5 + 5.7 = 15.2 miles.
b) They are 0.5 miles from Lake Lisa and 0.5 miles from the Roman ruins. So going back to the shop past Lake Lisa is 0.5 + 13.7 = 14.2 miles. Going back past the Roman Ruins and the Castle, but not the Waterfall is 0.5 + 3 + 11 = 14.5 miles. Going back past the Roman Ruins, the Castle and the Waterfall is 0.5 + 3 + 5.7 + 9.5 = 18.7 miles. So the shortest route is past Lake Lisa.

Page 19
Q5 a) It starts at 11 am and they need to be there at 10.30 am, so they should leave at 9.45 am at the latest.
b) The minibus costs £54 so it will cost them £54 ÷ 6 = £9 each.
c) Each person will pay 9 + 28 = £37.

Q6 a) To be in time for the Quick Flash Sale at 15.30, they need to see either the 11.00 or 11.30 showings of Snow Age. Both of these overlap with the 12.30 fashion show, so they have to go to the 10.00 fashion show. This finishes at 11.00, and it takes 20 minutes to get to the cinema, so they will only be able to make the 11.30 film showing.
10.00 — Fashion Show
11.30 — Snow Age
15.30 — Quick Flash Sale
b) The film finishes at 13.30, and it takes 20 minutes to walk to Bedhams, so they will arrive at 13.50. The sale starts at 15.30, so they have 1 h 40 mins for lunch.

Page 20
Q7 a) Cost = £5 entrance + (6 rides × £3 per ride) = £23.
b) Cost = £5 + (£3 × rides) + (£2 × photos).
If he has £40 to spend:
£40 = £5 + (£3 × 9) + (£2 × photos)
£40 = £32 + (£2 × photos)
£40 − £32 = (£2 × photos)
£8 = £2 × photos,
so number of photos = £8 ÷ £2 = 4 photos.

Answers (Foundation Level — The Basics): P.21 — P.24

Q8 Betty can either buy three single boat tickets, or two return tickets.
Single Tickets:
War Museum-Art Gallery: £3.75.
Art Gallery-Science Museum: £2.20.
Science Museum-War Museum: £4.50.
So total = £3.75 + £2.20 + £4.50 = £10.45.
Return Tickets:
Option 1: Return tickets between the War Museum and Art Gallery, and between the Art Gallery and Science Museum which costs £7 + £4 = £11. Option 2: Return tickets between the War Museum and Science Museum and between the War Museum and Art Gallery, which costs £8 + £4 = £12.
So it is cheaper to buy single tickets.
Total cost of boats and museum entry = £10.45 + £4.50 + £5.90 = £20.85.

Shopping
Page 21
Q1 a) 2 × 11 = 22 orange quarters for each team.
b) 22 for each team = 44 orange quarters. 44 ÷ 4 = 11 oranges in total.
c) 0.5 litres × 11 = 5.5 litres.
Q2 a) 11 × £15 = £165 for 11 shirts without a logo.
b) 11 × £20 = £220 for 11 shirts with a logo. Cath only has £200 so she can't afford the shirts.
c) 20% of £220 = 20 ÷ 100 × £220 = £44.
So it will cost £220 − £44 = £176 for the shirts with logos with the discount.

Page 22
Q3 a) £2.20 + £0.45 + £0.60 = £3.25, so she has been overcharged by 25p.
b) 1 chicken breast = £3.80, so half price = £3.80 ÷ 2 = £1.90. Emma should have been charged £3.80 + £1.90 = £5.70.

c) Emma has been overcharged £7.60 − £5.70 = £1.90 for the chicken and 25p for the meal deal. £1.90 + £0.25 = £2.15, so the cashier needs to refund her £2.15 in total.

Q4 Bread: 50% of £1.20 = 50 ÷ 100 × £1.20 = £0.60.
Milk: 25% of £0.80 = 25 ÷ 100 × £0.80 = £0.20.
Pasta: £1.30 ÷ 2 = £0.65.
Teabags: 20% of £2.40 = 20 ÷ 100 × £2.40 = £0.48.
Cereal: 10% of £2.20 = 10 ÷ 100 × £2.20 = £0.22.
Total saved = £0.60 + £0.20 + £0.65 + £0.48 + £0.22 = £2.15.

Page 23
Q5 a) MooveeWorld: £12 × 3 = £36 (plus free P&P).
b) Films4everyone: £30 + £4.50 = £34.50.
So John would save £36 − £34.50 = £1.50 using the offer from Films4everyone.
c) 10% of £36 = 10 ÷ 100 × £36 = £3.60. So it would cost £36 − £3.60 = £32.40, making it cheaper to get them from MooveeWorld rather than Films4everyone.

Q6 a) The shoes will have 10% off if Alison buys them on the store card. 10% of £70 = 10 ÷ 100 × £70 = £7.
£70 − £7 = £63, so today they will cost £63.
b) In a month's time she will have to pay 5% interest on the £63. 5% of £63 = 5 ÷ 100 × £63 = £3.15.
In total she will pay £63 + £3.15 = £66.15.
c) The shoes will have 5% off if Alison buys them today without a store card.
5% of £70 = 5 ÷ 100 × £70 = £3.50. £70 − £3.50 = £66.50, so it is cheaper to open the store card and pay £66.15.

Page 24
Q7 a) Tinned Food:
Between them, the 2 dogs will eat:
2 dogs × $\frac{3}{4}$ tins × 7 days × 2 weeks = $\frac{84}{4}$ = 21 tins.
Mixer:
The 2 dogs will eat:
2 dogs × 250 g × 7 days × 2 weeks = 7000 g of Mixer.
10 kg = 10 000 g, so Pete will need to buy 1 bag.
b) Tins: 21 × £1.24 = £26.04.
Bag: £25.80.
So Jenny should give Pete: £26.04 + £25.80 = £51.84.

Q8 Whitey Whites:
Box contains 15 tabs, with 1 tab needed per wash, so does 15 washes.
£5.10 ÷ 15 = £0.34 = 34p per wash.
Soapy Suds:
Box contains 20 tabs, with 1 tab needed per wash, so does 20 washes.
£6.20 ÷ 20 = £0.31 = 31p per wash.
Eco-wash:
Box contains 28 tabs, with 2 tabs needed per wash, so does 28 ÷ 2 = 14 washes.
£5.60 ÷ 14 = £0.40 = 40p per wash.
Soapy Suds costs the least per wash, so it is the best value for money.

ANSWERS (FOUNDATION LEVEL — THE BASICS)

Answers (Foundation Level — The Basics):   P.25 — P.30

Jobs
Page 25
Q1 a) Monday: 3 hours. Wednesday: 2 hours. Sunday: 4 hours.
Total: 2 + 3 + 4 = 9 hours.
b) 9 hours × £5.50 per hour = £49.50.

Q2 a) For office work:
6 shifts × 4 hours per shift = 24 hours per week.
Phil would get paid 24 hours × £4.50 per hour = £108 per week.
b) For factory work:
3 shifts × 12 hours per shift = 36 hours per week. So he would get paid 36 hours × £6 per hour = £216 per week.
This is £216 − £108 = £108 per week more than he would get working in an office.

Page 26
Q3 a) £56 ÷ 7 days = £8 per paper round.
b) Ben does 2 paper rounds per week and Charlie does 7 − 2 = 5 rounds per week. They get paid £8 per round, so Ben gets £8 × 2 = £16, and Charlie gets £8 × 5 = £40.

Q4 a) Each holiday will cost £2500 + £300 + £60 = £2860.
b) Polly should charge £2860 + £260 = £3120 for a week long holiday.
c) Each person should pay £3120 ÷ 15 = £208.

Page 27
Q5 a) Mean salaries:
Biologist:
(£30 000 + £28 000 + £32 000) ÷ 3 = £30 000.
Chemist:
(£34 000 + £52 000 + £25 000) ÷ 3 = £37 000.
Physicist:
(£48 000 + £28 000 + £30 000) ÷ 3 = £35 333.
So the chemist has the highest mean salary.

b) Salary ranges:
Biologist:
£32 000 − £28 000 = £4000.
Chemist:
£52 000 − £25 000 = £27 000.
Physicist:
£48 000 − £28 000 = £20 000.
So the biologist jobs have the smallest range of salaries.

Q6 a) If she met all her targets, Jenny would get a 15% bonus:
15 ÷ 100 × £12 000 = £1800.
So, her total pay would be £12 000 + £1800 = £13 800 a year.
b) If Jenny worked for Fizgig fashions and met all her sales targets, she would get a 10% bonus:
10 ÷ 100 × £13 000 = £1300.
Her total pay would be £13 000 + £1300 = £14 300 a year. So Jenny would get paid £14 300 − £13 800 = £500 more each year working at Fizgig Fashions.

Page 28
Q7 a) Mean number of lessons = (12 + 13 + 11 + 14 + 10 + 18) ÷ 6 = 13 lessons per week.
b) 13 lessons × £10.50 per lesson = £136.50 per week.
c) There are 52 weeks in a year, so she will earn £136.50 × 52 = £7098 per year. So no, she can't earn £10 000 per year teaching music.

Q8 £16 000 − £6475 = £9525, so Danni will have to pay 20% of £9525.
20 ÷ 100 × £9525 = £1905 income tax each year.

Going Out
Page 29
Q1 a) Dee should arrive 30 mins after 20.15, which is 20.45.
b) Stef needs to leave by 10 mins before 20.45, which is 20.35.
c) They should tell Kay they will be there for 15 mins after 20.45, which is 21.00 or 9 pm.

Q2 a) £23.80 + £3 = £26.80 = £27 to the nearest pound.
b) £27 split between 3 girls = £27 ÷ 3 = £9 each.
c) They should each get £10 − £9 = £1 back in change.

Page 30
Q3 a) Buying individual tickets would cost:
Adults: 2 × £30 = £60
OAPs: £25
Students: £25
Children: £15
Total = £60 + £25 + £25 + £15 = £125.
A 'Group of 5' ticket costs £135, so it is cheaper to buy the tickets separately.
b) 50% off is the same as halving the price, so for the cheapest Circle seats the adult tickets would cost £30 ÷ 2 = £15.
So the lowest amount the family can pay is:
£15 + £15 + £25 + £25 + £15 = £95.

Q4 a) £20 ÷ 5 = £4, so Mr Robinson needs to choose a drink costing £4 or under. The only drink under £4 is the Cranberry Crush, so he can afford to order 5 of these.
b) The drinks will cost 5 × £3.95 = £19.75. This leaves £20.00 − £19.75 = £0.25 or 25p, so Mr Robinson will not have enough for a packet of sweets.

Answers (Foundation Level — The Basics): P.31 — P.36

Page 31
Q5 a) Hannah and Wayne should get the 1735 bus from Nauton Green which will get them to the cinema at 1755 in time for the 1800 film. They need to set off by 10 mins before this, which is 1725.
b) The film plus trailers will last 20 mins + 160 mins = 180 mins, or 3 hrs. Starting at 1800, it should finish at 2100. The last bus leaves Minsterbury High St. at 2125, so they should be in time to catch it.

Q6 a) 330 ml ÷ 100p = 3.3 ml per penny.
500 ml ÷ 200p = 2.5 ml per penny.
So the 330 ml can is better value for money.
b) 75 g × 2 = 150 g popcorn in total.
150 g ÷ 50 g = 3 small bags.
£1.30 × 3 = £3.90 for small bags.
150 g ÷ 75 g = 2 medium bags.
£2.25 × 2 = £4.50 for medium bags.
150 g ÷ 150 g = 1 large bag, costing £4.50.
So the lowest amount they could spend is £3.90 buying 3 small bags.

Page 32
Q7 a) 6 slices of pizza each is 24 slices in total. This means ordering either 4 small, 3 medium or 2 large pizzas.
4 small pizzas cost 4 × £5.50 = £22.
3 medium pizzas cost 3 × £7.50 = £22.50.
2 large pizzas cost 2 × £9.50 = £19.
So the lowest amount the boys could pay is £19 for 2 large pizzas.
b) The boys would need to order 2 lots of Meal Deal 1 to have enough pizza, so this would cost 2 × £10 = £20. They would need to order just one of Meal Deal 2 so this would cost £18, which is the cheapest option overall.

Q8 £37.70 is £38 to the nearest pound. 20% of £38 =
20 ÷ 100 × £38 = £7.60 tip.
Total amount = £38 + £7.60 = £45.60
The boys need to split £45.60 between 4: £45.60 ÷ 4 = £11.40 each.

Decorating
Page 33
Q1 a) 1 litre covers 12 m², so Teresa will need 48 m² ÷ 12 m² = 4 litres for one coat.
b) For three coats she will need 3 × 4 litres = 12 litres.
c) Each tin is 2 litres so she will need 12 ÷ 2 = 6 tins of paint.

Q2 a) Perimeter is 4 + 4 + 2 + 1 + 2 + 5 = 18 m.
b) The distance around the walls is 18 m, the width of the door is 1 m, so she needs 18 − 1 = 17 m.

Page 34
Q3 a) The area is 100 × 50 = 5000 cm².
b) 100 cm² costs £1, so 5000 cm² costs 5000 ÷ 100 = £50.

Q4 a) Each tin of paint costs approximately £10.
4 × £10 = £40.
b) Each pack of wallpaper paste costs approximately £5. Each roll of border costs approximately £8.
(2 × £5) + (3 × £8) = £34.
c) £40 + £34 = £74.

Page 35
Q5 a) Split the room into two rectangles and work out each of their areas:
6 × 5 = 30 m². 3 × 1 = 3 m².
Then add the areas together:
30 + 3 = 33 m².
b) The carpet costs £8 per m² so it will cost Daniel £8 × 33 = £264.

Q6 a) E.g.

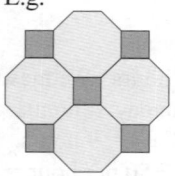

b) Area of square tiles = 5 cm × 5 cm × 20 tiles = 500 cm².
c) Area of octagonal tiles = 120.7 cm² × 20 tiles = 2414 cm².
d) Total = 500 + 2414 = 2914 cm² = 2900 cm² to the nearest 100 cm².

Page 36
Q7 a) James will need 0.5 × 36 = 18 litres of light blue paint.
b) Total number of parts in the ratio = 1 + 2 = 3.
Each part is 18 ÷ 3 = 6 litres of paint. James needs 2 parts white paint which is 6 × 2 = 12 litres. Each tin holds 2 litres so he needs 12 ÷ 2 = 6 tins.

Q8 a) Measured to the nearest 10 mm, it could be 10 mm ÷ 2 = 5 mm above or below the given value, so the smallest the gap could be is 620 mm − 5 mm = 615 mm.
b) Maximum oven widths:
SuperHeater: 620.5 mm.
OvenSolution: 614.5 mm.
Hot Oven: 615.5 mm.
The gap for the oven could be as small as 615 mm, so the OvenSolution is the only one that will definitely fit the gap.

Answers (Foundation Level — The Basics): P.37 — P.43

Gardening
Page 37
Q1 a) Total area is 9 × 12 = 108 m².
b) Area of flower bed is:
(12 − 5) × (9 − 5) = 7 × 4 = 28 m².
c) Area of turf needed is 108 − 28 = 80 m².

Q2 a) 10 × £4.75 = £47.50.
b) Delivery will cost £14.25 so it will cost Jordan £47.50 + £14.25 = £61.75.

Page 38
Q3 a) Area is 3 × 2 = 6 m².
b) e.g. Across the width he will need 3 m ÷ 0.5 m = 6 slabs, and across the length he will need 2 ÷ 0.5 m = 4 slabs, so in total Aftab will need 6 × 4 = 24 slabs.
c) Each slab costs 50p, so the total cost of the slabs is 24 × £0.50 = £12.

Q4 a) Perimeter is 3 + 2 + 3 + 2 = 10 m.
b) 10 m ÷ 0.5 m = 20 wooden blocks.
c) There are 15 blocks in each pack. 20 ÷ 15 = 1.3333... so Aftab needs to buy 2 packs, which will cost 2 × £5 = £10.

Page 39
Q5 a) The lawn is approximately triangular so its area is approximately $\frac{1}{2}$ × 10 × 8 = 40 m².
b) She needs 0.25 litres for 1 m² so for 40 m² she will need 0.25 × 40 = 10 litres.

Q6 For 75 ml of water, she would need 5 ml of lawn feed.
There is 7500 ml of water in the watering can so she will need:
(7500 ml ÷ 75 ml) × 5 ml
= 100 × 5 ml
= 500 ml of lawn feed.

Page 40
Q7 Measurements refer to what they should be on scale drawing:

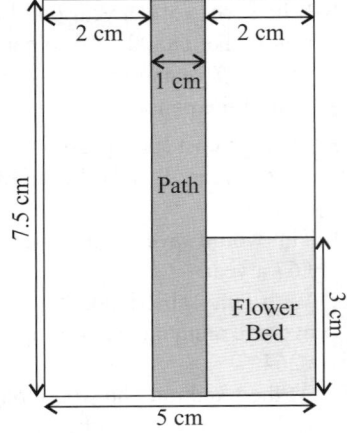

Q8 a) Circumference of pond
= π × Diameter
= π × 2 m = 6.28 m.
b) 6.28 m × 100 = 628 cm.
Number of tiles required = 628 cm ÷ 10 cm = 63 tiles to the nearest whole tile. Number of boxes = 63 tiles ÷ 10 tiles per box = 6.3, so Harry needs to buy 7 boxes of tiles.

City Planning
Page 41
Q1 a) 8.6 + 4.7 + 11.2 + 6.1 = 30.6 miles.
b) £2000 × 30.6 = £61 200.
c) At 2 days per mile, it should take 30.6 miles × 2 = 61.2 days.

Q2 a) The population of Cheddarville increased by 44 800 − 43 000 = 1800 between 2000 and 2005.
b) The population of Cheddarville increased by 46 600 − 44 800 = 1800 between 2005 and 2010.
c) The population is increasing by 1800 every 5 years, so in 2020, 10 years later, it will have increased to 46 600 + 1800 + 1800 = 50 200 people.

Page 42
Q3 a) Before the bypass:
16 038 cars and buses + 12 654 lorries and vans = 28 692 vehicles drove through Cowton each week.
b) After the bypass:
3216 cars and buses + 2540 lorries and vans = 5756 vehicles drove through Cowton each week.
This is 28 692 − 5756 = 22 936 fewer vehicles per day.

Q4 a) 35 000 vehicles drive through at the moment. 80 ÷ 100 × 35 000 = 28 000, so 28 000 fewer vehicles would drive through Sheepston each week if the bypass was built.
b) 28 000 cars would pay £3 each to use the bypass. 28 000 × £3 = £84 000 each week.
c) It would take:
£36 000 000 ÷ £84 000 per week = 429 weeks to pay off the cost of building the bypass. There are 52 weeks in a year, so it would take 429 ÷ 52 = 8.25 years, which is 8 years and 3 months.

Page 43
Q5 a) Building A:
Perimeter = 7 + 4 + 2 + 3 + 3 + 3 + 2 + 4 = 28 m.
Building B:
7 + 7 + 2 + 2 + 2 + 2 + 3 + 7 = 32 m.
b) The buildings are both 50 m high. Building A has a perimeter of 28 m so would need 50 m × 28 m = 1400 m² of glass. Building B has a perimeter of 32 m so would need 50 m × 32 m = 1600 m² of glass.

Answers (Foundation Level — The Basics): P.44 — P.48

Q6 Drawings not to scale,
Front Elevation:

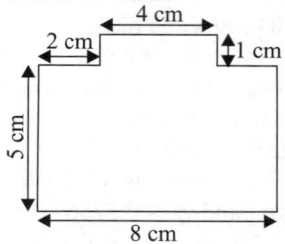

Side Elevation:

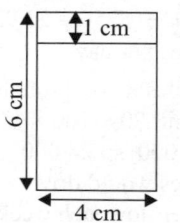

Plan:

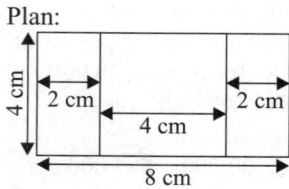

Page 44

Q7 a) E.g. Area = (20 m × 10 m) − (5 m × 4 m) = 200 − 20 = 180 m².
b) From the graph, 180 m² would cost £7000.

Q8 a) The houses that would be classed as low-cost are the ones in the categories £0 - £99 999 and £100 000 - £149 999. The total angle representing these categories is 60°. 60° ÷ 360° × 100% = 16.7%. This is less than the target of 25% so no, the New Housing Committee haven't met their target.
b) 25% of 1500 is 25 ÷ 100 × 1500 = 375 houses.

Paying Bills
Page 45

Q1 a) Tim will have to pay £12 000 − £3500 = £8500.
b) If he saves £500 a year on bills it will take £8500 ÷ £500 per year = 17 years to pay for the cost of the panels.

Q2 a) Average cost for 1 person = £156 a year. £156 ÷ 12 = £13 a month.
b) Tim would save £223 − £156 = £67 a year.
c) With Tim's girlfriend, the average annual cost goes up to £264.
At the fixed rate, he would pay £223 a year, so it is cheaper to stick with the fixed rate.

Page 46

Q3 a) Lucy should have been charged 50 × £12.99 = £649.50 for the buffet.
b) Total cost = £250 + £649.50 = £899.50.
Minus deposit: £899.50 − £200 = £699.50.
Half this amount: £699.50 ÷ 2 = £349.75. So Lucy needs to pay £349.75 by 1st May.

Q4 a) The first 325 units cost 16p per unit = 325 × £0.16 = £52.
Remaining units = (478 − 325) = 153 units. These are charged at 11p per unit = 153 × 0.11 = £16.83.
Total before VAT = £16.83 + £52 = £68.83.
b) VAT at 5% of £68.83 = 5 ÷ 100 × £68.83 = £3.44, so total cost = £68.83 + £3.44 = £72.27.

Page 47

Q5 a) Repair cost = 155 + 75 + 85 + 210 + 35 + 95 = £655.
b) 15% of £995 = 15 ÷ 100 × £995 = £149.25. So the value of the car is: £995 − £149.25 = £845.75. It will cost £655 to get the car fixed, so no, she will not have to pay more than the car is worth.

Q6 In September, Jane used 90 minutes call time and 130 text messages.
TextyText:
Call cost = (90 − 30 mins) × £0.15 per min = £9.
Text cost = £0 (all included).
Line rental = £14.
Total = £9 + £14 = £23.
TextyTalk:
Call cost = £0 (all included).
Text cost = (130 − 50) × £0.10 per text = £8.
Line rental = £18.
Total = £8 + £18 = £26.
So Jane should go on TextyText tariff for the lowest monthly bill.

In the News
Page 48

Q1 a) There are 20 giant toads in the park.
b) There are 16 normal toads in the park.
c) The scale on the bar chart does not start at zero, so it looks like there are 5 times more giant toads than normal toads from the sizes of the bars on show.

Q2 a) 'Eyes': 42 + 13 + 11 + 88 + 49 = 203 mins.
Arthur: 55 + 17 + 44 + 19 + 45 = 180 mins.
So 'Eyes' has the longest total stare time.
b) 'Eyes' McGregor has won 4 out of his previous 5 games, and Arthur 'The Unblinkable' has won 3 out of 5, so 'Eyes' McGregor is more likely to win.

Answers (Foundation Level — The Basics): P.49 — P.53

Page 49

Q3 a) $\frac{3}{4}$ of the pie chart represents people who said MDobz were the best. As a percentage, $\frac{3}{4}$ of 100% = 75%.

b) 20 people voted in total, so $\frac{3}{4} \times 20 = 15$ people.

c) Any two reasons from e.g. there are not enough people in the sample / the question is leading / they have only asked people who read their website so are likely to agree with their opinions / the answers to choose from are not clear.

Q4 a) Add the house prices together: 120 000 + 100 000 + 95 000 + 110 000 + 98 000 = £523 000. Then divide by the number of houses: 523 000 ÷ 5 = £104 600.

b) Add the house prices together: 75 000 + 60 000 + 160 000 + 95 000 + 155 000 = £545 000. Then divide by the number of houses: 545 000 ÷ 5 = £109 000.

c) Range of prices in Trundle: 120 000 − 95 000 = £25 000. Range of prices in Udderston: 160 000 − 60 000 = £100 000. So there is a greater range of house prices in Udderston.

Page 50

Q5 a) Layla's survey is more reliable because e.g. she asked more people / has a bigger sample / she carried out her survey at the weekend when people who are both employed and unemployed are likely to be in town / she stood in the centre of town rather than outside the job centre which is likely to have more people around who are unemployed.

b) Layla's survey found that 5% of people were unemployed. 5% of 20 000 = 5 ÷ 100 × 20 000 = 1000 people.

Q6 Big City:
Angle of sector unemployed = 90°. 90° ÷ 360° × 1 000 000 = 250 000 people unemployed.
Localville:
Angle of sector unemployed = 120°. 120° ÷ 360° × 9000 = 3000 people unemployed.

Health and Fitness
Page 51

Q1 a) 3 months gym membership is £35 × 3 = £105.

b) Each month Laura could save: (£25 + £35) − £45 = £60 − £45 = £15.

Q2 a)

Number of pieces of fruit	Tally	Frequency
0	IIII	5
1	IIII III	8
2	IIII	4
3	IIII IIII	10
4	II	2
5	I	1

b) Rick asked 5 + 8 + 4 + 10 + 2 + 1 = 30 people.

c) 3 pieces of fruit.

Page 52

Q3 a) Ribble Rovers:
Won 12 so: 12 × 3 = 36.
Drawn 2 so: 2 × 1 = 2.
Total number of points is 36 + 2 = 38.
Duddon Dragons:
Won 13 so: 13 × 3 = 39.
Drawn 2 so: 2 × 1 = 2.
Total number of points is 39 + 2 = 41.

b) Ribble Rovers gain 3 extra points so have 41 points. Duddon Dragons gain no extra points so also have 41 points.

Q4 a) Mark has scored 59 + 42 + 38 = 139 runs.
Ryan has scored 56 + 50 + 42 = 148 runs.
Peter has scored 72 + 41 + 49 = 162 runs.
So Peter has scored the most runs in total.

b) Mark's mean score is 139 ÷ 3 = 46.3 runs.
Ryan's mean score is 148 ÷ 3 = 49.3 runs.
Peter's mean score is 162 ÷ 3 = 54 runs.
So Peter has the highest mean score.

Page 53

Q5 a) E.g. once a month or less, 1-3 times a month, 4-6 times a month, more than 6 times a month.

b) E.g. she could post the questionnaire to all the members.

c) E.g. she could say that everyone who returns the questionnaire will go into a prize draw.

Q6

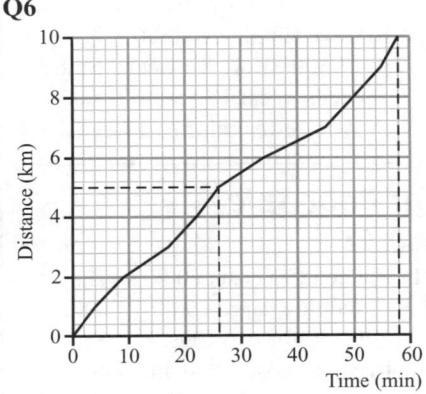

a) It took Steve 58 mins to complete the race.

b) Reading from the graph, the first 5 km took 26 mins and the second 5 km took 32 mins so no, Steve is not right.

Answers (Foundation Level — The Basics): P.54 — P.59

Page 54

Q7 a)

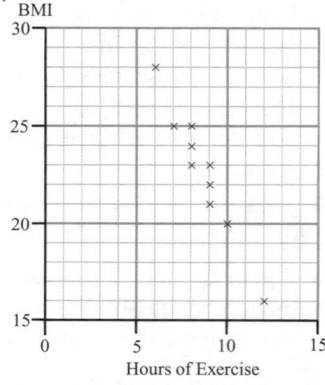

b) The more time spent exercising the lower a person's BMI.

Q8 a) Total number of calories is 2700 + 2550 + 2450 + 2650 + 2500 + 2750 + 2950 = 18 550. Mean number of calories is 18 550 ÷ 7 = 2650.

b) Clive should eat 2500 × 7 = 17 500 calories a week. So he needs to eat 18 550 − 17 500 = 1050 fewer calories a week.

Car Boot Sale
Page 55

Q1 a) Each CD costs £0.80 so she should charge £0.80 + £0.80 = £1.60 for two CDs.

b) Books cost £0.80 and teddy bears cost £1.30 so she should charge £0.80 + £1.30 = £2.10.

c) Books and CDs cost £0.80 each, the hairdryer costs £2.50 and the scarf costs £1.20, so she should charge: £0.80 + £0.80 + £2.50 + £1.20 = £5.30.

Q2 a) An umbrella and a watch will cost £2.75 + £5.10 = £7.85. Nick should give him £10 − £7.85 = £2.15 change.

b) A teapot and a watch will cost £1.39 + £5.10 = £6.49. Nick should give him £7 − £6.49 = £0.51 change (51p).

Page 56

Q3 Gloves: £1.70
Toaster: £2.50
Bracelets: 80p
Leg warmers: £1.40
DVDs: £1.30
Play-pen: £8.00

Q4 a) Cushions are £2.80 each but Dave would get the third cushion free so it would cost him £2.80 + £2.80 = £5.60.

b) Cushions are £2.40 each but Dave would get one for half price (£1.20) so it would cost him £2.40 + £2.40 + £1.20 = £6.

c) The cheapest cushions cost £5.60 so Dave should get £20 − £5.60 = £14.40 change. So no, he has not been given the right amount of change.

Page 57

Q5 a) Volume = length × width × height = 40 × 50 × 20 = 40 000 cm^3.

b) Volume = 100 × 80 × 40 = 320 000 cm^3.

c) He will be able to fit 320 000 ÷ 40 000 = 8 boxes into each crate.

Q6 a) Jonny has 3 of the 12 books so needs to buy 9 books. Each book is £0.75 so this will cost him £0.75 × 9 = £6.75. So it's cheaper for him to buy the whole set.

b) Jonny has £8, he's spent £6 on books so has £8 − £6 = £2 left. Marbles cost £0.45 each. £2 ÷ £0.45 = 4.44... so he can buy 4 marbles.

Page 58

Q7 a) Computer games:
15 ÷ 100 × £3.00 = £0.45.
Video Player:
15 ÷ 100 × £5.00 = £0.75.
Badminton Racket:
15 ÷ 100 × £2.00 = £0.30.
Shoes:
15 ÷ 100 × £1.20 = £0.18.
Mug:
15 ÷ 100 × £0.80 = £0.12.

b) Computer games:
£3 − £0.45 = £2.55.
Video Player:
£5 − £0.75 = £4.25.
Badminton Racket:
£2 − £0.30 = £1.70.
Shoes:
£1.20 − £0.18 = £1.02.
Mug:
£0.80 − £0.12 = £0.68.

Q8 a) It cost Jess £15.05 + £15.75 + £9.70 = £40.50 in total.

b) 20% of £40.50 = 20 ÷ 100 × £40.50 = £8.10. So Jess would need to sell all the necklaces for £40.50 + £8.10 = £48.60. So she needs to sell each necklace for £48.60 ÷ 15 = £3.24.

Banking
Page 59

Q1 a) After the triplets' 18th birthday there will be:
£300 + (18 × £100) = £300 + £1800 = £2100.

b) £2100 ÷ 3 = £700 each.

Q2 a) Matthew has approximately £2400 to last 6 months, so he should only spend around £2400 ÷ 6 = £400 each month.

b) Matthew has approximately £900 to last him 3 months, which leaves around £900 ÷ 3 = £300 per month.

c) In his final year Matthew will have an increase of 10% on approximately £400 per month. 10% of £400 = 10 ÷ 100 × £400 = £40. So he will have around £400 + £40 = £440 to spend each month.

Answers (Foundation Level — The Basics): P.60 — P.62

Page 60

Q3 a) PGS Bank would pay 20% of £100 = £20.
b) Lomond Bank would pay ¼ of what he pays in, which is the same as 25%. This is more than the 20% offered by PGS, so his best deal is with Lomond Bank.

Q4 a) Dylan met the target in January, February and May.
b) As he met the target in three of the months, he should get: £10 × 3 = £30.

Page 61

Q5 a) The bank will lend Sean: 2.5 × £20 000 = £50 000.
b) One fifth of £55 000 = £55 000 ÷ 5 = £11 000. So he needs £11 000 − £10 000 = £1000 more.

Q6 a) £1500 ÷ £120 = 12.5, so it will take 13 months to save £1500.
b) Sean needs to save at least £1500 ÷ 6 months = £250 per month.

Page 62

Q7 a) At the end of one year there will be £2000 + (4% of £2000) in the account.
4% of £2000 = 4 ÷ 100 × £2000 = £80, so total = £2000 + £80 = £2080.
b) After the first year there will be £2080 in the account.
At the end of the second year there will be
£2080 + (4% of £2080) = £2080 + (4 ÷ 100 × £2080) = £2080 + £83.20 = £2163.20 in the account.

Q8 a) Annual interest rate on a loan of £6750 is 15%.
15% of £6750 = 15 ÷ 100 × £6750 = £1012.50.
Total to pay back = £6750 + £1012.50 = £7762.50.
b) Each month, Emily will have to pay £7762.50 ÷ 12 months
= £646.875
= £646.88 to the nearest penny.

Guide to Themes and Topics
Foundation Level

Party 1
    Q1: *Arithmetic*
    Q2: *Arithmetic, Proportion*
    Q3: *Two-way Tables*
    Q4: *Time*
    Q5: *Probability*
    Q6: *Formulas, Percentages, Financial Arithmetic*
    Q7: *Enlargements and Scale Factors, Nets, Volume of 3D Shapes*
    Q8: *Conversion Factors (Metric-Imperial), Calculating Averages*

Holidays 5
    Q1: *Bar-Line Graphs*
    Q2: *Conversion Factors (Currency)*
    Q3: *Inequalities, Arithmetic*
    Q4: *Bar Charts, Line Graphs*
    Q5: *Two-way Tables, Financial Arithmetic*
    Q6: *Bar Charts*
    Q7: *Timings and Timetables*
    Q8: *Two-way Tables, Financial Arithmetic*
    Q9: *Inequalities, Financial Arithmetic, Two-way Tables*

Transport 9
    Q1: *Financial Arithmetic*
    Q2: *Timings and Timetables*
    Q3: *Financial Arithmetic, Fractions*
    Q4: *Time, Financial Arithmetic*
    Q5: *Maps and Scale Drawings, Conversion Factors (Metric-Imperial), Compound Measures (Speed)*
    Q6: *Time, Compound Measures (Speed)*

Food and Drink 12
    Q1: *Scales and Measurements, Arithmetic*
    Q2: *Scales and Measurements, Fractions, Conversion Factors (Imperial Units)*
    Q3: *Ratios*
    Q4: *Proportion*
    Q5: *Conversion Factors (Metric-Imperial), Formulas, Fractions*
    Q6: *Conversion Factors (Metric-Imperial), Volume of 3D Shapes*
    Q7: *Time*
    Q8: *Ratios*

Guide to Themes and Topics
Foundation Level

Day Trip **16**
    Q1: *Timings and Timetables*
    Q2: *Financial Arithmetic, Time*
    Q3: *Financial Arithmetic*
    Q4: *Fractions, Compound Measures (Speed)*
    Q5: *Compound Measures (Speed), Arithmetic*
    Q6: *Timings and Timetables*
    Q7: *Financial Arithmetic, Percentages*
    Q8: *Formulas, Financial Arithmetic*

Shopping **20**
    Q1: *Financial Arithmetic (Non-Calculator)*
    Q2: *Financial Arithmetic*
    Q3: *Fractions, Conversion Factors (Metric Units), Financial Arithmetic*
    Q4: *Fractions, Conversion Factors (Metric Units), Financial Arithmetic*
    Q5: *Financial Arithmetic, Two-way Tables*
    Q6: *Financial Arithmetic, Percentages*
    Q7: *Best Buys*
    Q8: *Percentages, Area*

Jobs **24**
    Q1: *Calculating Averages and Spread, Rounding*
    Q2: *Ratios, Financial Arithmetic*
    Q3: *Financial Arithmetic*
    Q4: *Financial Arithmetic*
    Q5: *Financial Arithmetic, Rounding*
    Q6: *Percentages, Financial Arithmetic*
    Q7: *Financial Arithmetic, Percentages*
    Q8: *Financial Arithmetic, Percentages*

Going Out **28**
    Q1: *Time*
    Q2: *Financial Arithmetic (Non-Calculator)*
    Q3: *Financial Arithmetic (Non-Calculator), Percentages*
    Q4: *Financial Arithmetic (Non-Calculator)*
    Q5: *Financial Arithmetic (Non-Calculator), Percentages, Rounding*
    Q6: *Timings and Timetables*
    Q7: *Best Buys*
    Q8: *Percentages, Financial Arithmetic*
    Q9: *Formulas, Financial Arithmetic*

Guide to Themes and Topics
Foundation Level

Decorating 32
    Q1: *Calculation Bounds, Rounding*
    Q2: *Area, Financial Arithmetic*
    Q3: *Ratios*
    Q4: *Tessellation, Area*
    Q5: *Perimeter, Financial Arithmetic*
    Q6: *Area, Financial Arithmetic*
    Q7: *Area*
    Q8: *Area, Perimeter, Estimating*

Gardening 36
    Q1: *Area, Perimeter*
    Q2: *Area, Perimeter*
    Q3: *Estimating, Area, Ratios*
    Q4: *Area, Estimating*
    Q5: *Scale Drawings, Loci and Constructions*
    Q6: *Scale Drawings, Loci and Constructions, Perimeter*
    Q7: *Circumference*
    Q8: *Volume of 3D Shapes, Proportion*

City Planning 40
    Q1: *Perimeter, Area*
    Q2: *Projections, Scale Drawings, Area*
    Q3: *Percentages*
    Q4: *Bar Charts, Percentages, Sampling and Data Collection*
    Q5: *Pie Charts, Fractions*
    Q6: *Number Patterns*
    Q7: *Pythagoras' Theorem*
    Q8: *Area, Percentages, Financial Arithmetic*

Paying Bills 44
    Q1: *Financial Arithmetic, Percentages, Calculating Averages*
    Q2: *Financial Arithmetic*
    Q3: *Straight Line Graphs*
    Q4: *Financial Arithmetic, Percentages*
    Q5: *Financial Arithmetic, Percentages*
    Q6: *Financial Arithmetic*
    Q7: *Financial Arithmetic, Percentages, Two-way Tables*
    Q8: *Financial Arithmetic, Percentages*

Guide to Themes and Topics
Foundation Level

In the News **48**
    Q1: *Pie Charts, Sampling and Data Collection*
    Q2: *Calculating Averages*
    Q3: *Pie Charts, Sampling and Data Collection*
    Q4: *Bar Charts, Pie Charts*
    Q5: *Probability, Calculating Averages*
    Q6: *Calculating Averages and Spread*

Health and Fitness **51**
    Q1: *Sampling and Data Collection*
    Q2: *Frequency Tables, Arithmetic*
    Q3: *Scatter Graphs and Correlation*
    Q4: *Calculating Averages, Arithmetic*
    Q5: *Distance-time Graphs, Compound Measures (Speed)*
    Q6: *Two-way Tables, Calculating Averages and Spread*
    Q7: *Financial Arithmetic*
    Q8: *Distance-time Graphs, Compound Measures (Speed)*

Car Boot Sale **55**
    Q1: *Financial Arithmetic (Non-Calculator)*
    Q2: *Financial Arithmetic (Non-Calculator)*
    Q3: *Financial Arithmetic (Non-Calculator)*
    Q4: *Percentages, Rounding*
    Q5: *Financial Arithmetic, Percentages*
    Q6: *Straight Line Graphs, Formulas*
    Q7: *Formulas, Financial Arithmetic, Two-way Tables*
    Q8: *Financial Arithmetic, Fractions*

Banking **59**
    Q1: *Financial Arithmetic, Percentages, Fractions*
    Q2: *Financial Arithmetic*
    Q3: *Percentages, Financial Arithmetic*
    Q4: *Financial Arithmetic*
    Q5: *Percentages, Financial Arithmetic*
    Q6: *Financial Arithmetic, Percentages, Rounding, Two-way Tables*
    Q7: *Powers, Decimals, Formulas*
    Q8: *Powers, Decimals, Formulas, Trial and Improvement*

Answers (Foundation Level): P.1 — P.4

Party

Page 1

Q1 a) 32 chocolate bars split into 12 bags is 32 ÷ 12 = 2.666... bars. So she can put 2 chocolate bars in each bag.
b) 90 rubber animals split into 12 bags is 90 ÷ 12 = 7.5 animals. So she can put 7 animals in each bag.
c) Number of animals left is 90 − 9 = 81. 81 split into 12 bags is 81 ÷ 12 = 6.75. So she can put 6 animals in each bag.

Q2 a) Number of slices of pizza needed is 15 × 3 = 45. There are 8 slices in each pizza so 45 ÷ 8 = 5.625. Rupert needs to buy 6 pizzas.
b) 15 people need 25 g of crisps each. 15 × 25 = 375 g. There are 300 g in a packet so he needs 2 packets.
c) 17 people need 2 rolls each, so Rupert needs 17 × 2 = 34 rolls. He has bought 8 packs of 4 rolls so has 8 × 4 = 32 rolls. So he doesn't have enough.

Page 2

Q3 a) and b)

	Game 1	Game 2	Game 3	Total
Team 1	5	5	5	15
Team 2	2	10	10	22
Team 3	10	2	2	14

c) If Team 1 had won game 3 they would have been given 10 points instead of 5 and would have a total score of 20. Team 2 would have been given a maximum of 5 points and so would have a maximum total score of 17. So yes, the overall result of the tournament would have been affected as Team 1 would have won.

Q4 a) The ham and peanut pizza should be taken out at 10:51 pm.
The squirrel pizza should be taken out at 10:58 pm.
b) The potato pizza goes into the oven at 10:51 pm. It is left in for 14 + 3 minutes so should be taken out at 11:08 pm.
c) The earliest time the cabbage pizza can go into the oven is 10:58 pm. It needs to cook for 17 mins so the earliest time it could be ready by is 11:15 pm.

Page 3

Q5 a) There are 21 cakes in total and 8 fish sauce flavoured ones, so the probability that Ken will pick a fish sauce flavoured cake is 8/21.
b) There are 20 cakes left and 7 of them are fish sauce flavoured so the probability that Ken will pick another fishy one is 7/20 or 0.35. This is approximately a 1 in 3 chance, so Chris is wrong to say that it's highly unlikely that Ken will pick a second fishy cake.
c) There are 19 cakes left and 6 fishy ones. The probability that Chris will pick a fishy cake is 6/19 or 0.32, which is less than the probability was when Ken took his, so Chris is right.

Q6 a) Total cost = £100 for the room + £150 for the disco + £5 per person for food. So for n people, the total cost, C, is: C = £250 + £5 × n
C = 250 + 5n
b) If the total cost can be no more than £500, then:
500 = 250 + 5n
500 − 250 = 5n
250 = 5n, so
n = 250 ÷ 5 = 50
So he can have no more than 50 people at the party.
c) Total cost = 250 + (5 × 40) = £450. So Ed would have to pay a deposit of 10 ÷ 100 × £450 = £45.

Page 4

Q7 a) Each length needs to be multiplied by 5, so the new dimensions are:
length: 10 × 5 = 50 cm
width: 3 × 5 = 15 cm
height: 2.5 × 5 = 12.5 cm.
b) E.g.

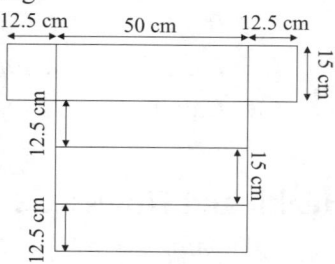

c) Volume of chocolate needed is 50 × 15 × 12.5 = 9375 cm³.

Q8 a) 1 kg ≈ 2.2 lbs, so Tim weighs 86 × 2.2 ≈ 189 lbs.
Nick weighs 70 × 2.2 ≈ 154 lbs.
b) Work out the total weight of each team so far in lbs (1 st = 14 lbs):
Team 1
James: 11 × 14 = 154 lbs.
Cooper: 10 × 14 + 5 = 145 lbs.
Simon: 13 × 14 + 8 = 190 lbs.
Total = 154 + 145 + 190 = 489 lbs.
Team 2
Frank: 9 × 14 + 4 = 130 lbs.
Joe: 10 × 14 + 11 = 151 lbs.
Tim: 189 lbs (from part a).
Total = 130 + 151 + 189 = 470 lbs.
Find Mark and Nick's weights in lbs:
Mark: 9 × 14 + 7 = 133 lbs.
Nick: 154 lbs (from part a).
Team 1 is heavier than Team 2 so try adding Mark to Team 1 and Nick to Team 2 (as Mark is lighter) and calculate the mean weights to the nearest lb:
Team 1
(489 + 133) ÷ 4 = 156 lbs.
Team 2
(470 + 154) ÷ 4 = 156 lbs.
So Mark should join Team 1 and Nick should join Team 2.

ANSWERS (FOUNDATION LEVEL)

Answers (Foundation Level): P.5 — P.10

Holidays
Page 5
Q1 She should choose Mont Pont in February and Val d'Essert in October.

Q2 300 Euros × £0.87 = £261.

Q3 a) 19.4 + 12.5 + 3.2 = 35.1 kg.
b) Maximum Total allowance = 15 + 5 + 15 = 35 kg, so Lola has too much luggage and she won't be able to repack her bags to be within the limits.

Page 6
Q4 a) June, July, August and September.
b) Of the months with the right temperature, July has the lowest rainfall so they should plan the holiday for July.

Q5 a) Two weeks in April will cost:
(2 × £250) + (2 × £125) = £750.
One week in June will cost:
(2 × £270) + (2 × £135) = £810.
So it is cheaper to go for two weeks in April.
b) For full board, two weeks in April will cost:
(2 × £330) + (2 × £165) = £990.
One week in June will cost:
(2 × £300) + (2 × £150) = £900.
So they could only afford to go for one week in June.

Page 7
Q6 Prices for flights out:
8th: £65
9th: £45
10th: £40
11th: £35
Prices for corresponding return flights:
15th: £50
16th: £40
17th: £30
18th: £45
So cheapest pair is the 10th and 17th at £40 + £30 = £70.

Q7 a) They need to arrive 2 hours before 1300 = 1100, so the best train is the 0956 from Chorley to get in at 1047.
b) The train leaves Bolton at 1008, so Ben needs to set off 20 mins before this — at 0948.
c) The next train for Ben gets in at 1117. This is 1 hour and 43 mins before departure time so he will make it in time.

Page 8
Q8 a) Need Oak Cabin for 2 nights at £150 per night. Total cost = (£150 × 2 nights) + £150 for food and drink = £450.
Each person will owe £450 ÷ 6 = £75.
b) Total budget = £80 × 4 = £320. They can now book the Ash Cabin at £125 a night, so cabin cost = £125 × 2 = £250. This leaves £320 − £250 = £70 for food and drink.

Q9 a) Cost with Surfsup:
£26 + £23 + (2 × £15) + (2 × £45) + (2 × £20) = £209.
Cost with WaveGday:
£80 + £75 + (2 × £18) = £191.
Cost with FlyBeach:
£63 + £52 + (2 × £5) + (2 × 5 kg × £3) + (2 × £25) = £205.
So the least amount she can spend on flights is £191 with WaveGday.
b) Kelly can only save money by reducing the weight of her luggage. Doing this won't change the cost of the WaveGday flights so they are still too expensive; and with FlyBeach even reducing her luggage to below 20 kg would still cost
£63 + £52 + (2 × £5) + (2 × £25) = £175.
So the only way to fly within her budget is to reduce her luggage to 15 kg and fly with Surfsup, at a cost of:
£26 + £23 + (2 × £15) + (2 × £20) + (2 × £20) = £159.

Transport
Page 9
Q1 a) Each day involves a return journey so
2 × (30 + 34 + 28 + 39 + 40) = 2 × 171 = 342 miles.
b) 342 miles × £0.22 per mile = £75.24.
c) £0.22 − £0.13 = £0.09 per mile extra. For a week travelling 300 miles Sophie would get £0.09 × £300 = £27 extra.

Q2 a) Colin wants to be there 10 minutes before 11.00, which is 10.50. He needs to start walking from the bus station 15 minutes before this, at 10.35, so he should get the bus that arrives at the bus station at 10.25, which leaves Longridge at 09.31.
b) The next bus gets in at 10.40, so with a 15 minute walk he will get there at 10.55, which is still in time for his 11.00 interview.

Page 10
Q3 a) Driving will cost:
(£55 × 1.5) + £76 = £158.50.
The train will cost:
£98 × 2 = £196.
Flying will cost:
(£29.99 × 2) + (£34.99 × 2) = £59.98 + £69.98 = £129.96.
So flying is the cheapest option.
b) Railcard will save them $\frac{1}{3}$ of £196 = £196 ÷ 3 = £65.33. So the train will cost £196 − £65.33 = £130.66 in total with the discount, which is still not as cheap as flying.

Q4 a) If Caroline gets the ferry, she will get there 3h 15 mins after 19.30, i.e. 22.45 (10.45 pm). If she flies, she will get there at 55 mins after 19.55, i.e. 20.50 (8.50 pm). So the earliest time she could arrive is 8.50 pm.

Answers (Foundation Level): P.11 — P.14

b) Going to Dublin, the train and ferry cost £20.20 + £26 = £46.20.
The train and flight cost £14.30 + £32.99 = £47.29, so the ferry is cheaper.
Coming back to Chester, the ferry and train cost £32 + £20.20 = £52.20.
The flight and train cost £35.40 + £14.30 = £49.70, so the flight is cheaper. Caroline should take the ferry out and fly back, costing her £46.20 + £49.70 = £95.90 in total.

c) The ferry departs at 19.30. Leaving 40 minutes to check in, she needs to arrive in Holyhead at 18.50.
The train takes 1 hr 45 mins, so the latest she can catch it is 17.05.

Page 11
Q5 a) 1 cm on map = 100 000 cm.
100 000 cm ÷ 100 = 1000 m.
1000 m = 1 km,
so 1 cm on map is 1 km.
16 cm on map is 16 km.
1.6 km ≈ 1 mile,
so 16 km ≈ 10 miles.

b) Time = Distance ÷ Speed.
= 10 miles ÷ 60 mph = $\frac{1}{6}$ hour
= $\frac{1}{6}$ × 60 minutes = 10 minutes.

Q6 a) The family need to drive 225 miles to Folkestone.
Time = Distance ÷ Speed
= 225 miles ÷ 50 mph
= 4.5 hrs = 4 hrs 30 mins.
They need to set off 4 hrs 30 mins before 10.30 — at 06.00.

b) They will arrive at the campsite 6 hours 35 minutes after 10.35 — at 17.10 UK time. France is 1 hour ahead of UK time, so this will be 18.10 French time.

Food and Drink
Page 12
Q1 a) 170 g lentils needed so use: 100 g + 50 g + 20 g.

b) Four carrots weigh 300 g. This is half the amount needed, so Jo needs 4 more carrots.

c) Each division on the scale is 100 ml ÷ 4 = 25 ml. Jug scale reads 125 ml, so she needs 150 ml − 125 ml = 25 ml more.

Q2 a) Each division on the scale is 1 oz. The scale reads 10 oz, but it should read 6½ + 4½ = 11 oz, so he needs 1 oz more.

b) Flour and sugar = 11 oz, so with butter the weight should be 11 oz + 5½ oz = 16½ oz, or 1 lb and ½ oz.

c) From the scale, 1¾ lb = 28 oz. Half of this = 28 ÷ 2 = 14 oz.

Page 13
Q3 a) Jake has 3 × 1 litre = 3 litres orange. If this is 3 parts in the recipe, then 1 part = 1 litre. He needs 2 parts pineapple juice = 2 litres. He needs 1 part ginger ale = 1 litre.

b) Split 3 litres in the ratio 3 : 2 : 1.
No. of parts = 3 + 2 + 1 = 6.
Each part = 3 litres ÷ 6 = ½ litre.
Orange juice:
3 parts × ½ litre = 1½ litres.
Pineapple juice:
2 parts × ½ litre = 1 litre.
Ginger ale:
1 part × ½ litre = ½ litre.

c) 3 litres = 3000 ml.
3000 ml ÷ 24 = 125 ml per person.

Q4 For 24 people, Jake needs to scale up the recipes as follows:
Sausage Rolls: Multiply by 4.
Cheesy Biscuits: Multiply by 3.
Cupcakes: Multiply by 2.
Ingredients for Sausage Rolls:
4 × 600 g = 2400 g sausage meat
4 × 1 = 4 small onions
4 × 450 g = 1800 g pastry
4 × 1 = 4 eggs

Ingredients for Cheesy Biscuits:
3 × 100 g = 300 g flour
3 × 100 g = 300 g butter
3 × 100 g = 300 g cheese
3 × 1 = 3 eggs
Ingredients for Cupcakes:
2 × 125 g = 250 g butter
2 × 275 g = 550 g sugar
2 × 2 = 4 eggs
2 × 125 ml = 250 ml milk
2 × 200 g = 400 g flour
Total ingredients list:
2400 g sausage meat
4 small onions
1800 g pastry
11 eggs
700 g flour
550 g butter
300 g cheese
550 g sugar
250 ml milk.
Jake already has enough onions, cheese, sugar and milk so he needs:
2400 g sausage meat
1800 g pastry
11 eggs
700 g flour
550 g butter

Page 14
Q5 a) Butter ≈ ½ lb × 450
= 225 g.
Sugar ≈ ¾ lb × 450
= 338 g to the nearest g.

b) 1 litre = 1000 ml, so:
Milk ≈ ¼ pint ÷ 1.75 × 1000
= 140 ml.

c) °C = $\frac{5}{9}$(325 − 32) = 160 °C to nearest 10 °C.

Q6 1 inch ≈ 2.5 cm, so the ideal tin would be 8 × 2.5 = 20 cm square, and 2 × 2.5 = 5 cm deep.
This would have a volume of 20 × 20 × 5 = 2000 cm³.
Rectangular tin:
Volume = 20 × 23 × 4 = 1840 cm³.
Round tin:
Radius = 20 cm ÷ 2 = 10 cm.
Volume = π × 10² × 7 = 2199.1 cm³.
The round tin is big enough, but the rectangular tin is too small, so Laura should use the round tin.

Answers (Foundation Level): P.15 — P.19

Page 15
Q7 a) Potatoes will take 20 mins + 50 mins = 70 mins to cook, plus 10 mins to peel.
Total time = 80 mins = 1 hour 20 mins.
To be ready at 1.30 pm he must start peeling at 12.10 pm.
b) Vegetable bake needs to stand for 5 mins, so he can cook the peas while bake is standing. Peas should go in at 1.25 pm and vegetable bake 13 mins before, at 1.12 pm.
c) Cooking time for the turkey: (4 kg × 45 mins per kg) + 20 mins = 200 mins. Needs to stand for 10 mins, so needs to start cooking 210 mins before 1.30 pm.
210 mins = 3 hours 30 mins, so turkey should be defrosted by 10.00 am. Defrosting will take 4 hours per kg = 16 hours. So Chloe needs to set her alarm for 6.00 pm on Saturday night.

Q8 Need 5 × 240 ml = 1200 ml coffee. Split in ratio 3 : 1.
No. of parts = 3 + 1 = 4.
Each part = 1200 ml ÷ 4 = 300 ml.
Milk = 3 parts = 3 × 300 ml = 900 ml.
Water for coffee = 1 part = 300 ml.
Ground coffee = 10 g × (300 ml ÷ 150 ml) = 20 g.

Day Trip
Page 16
Q1 a) The order should be: sea lions (10.30), polar bears (11.30), meerkats (12.00), monkeys (12.30), tigers (14.30), lions (15.30), penguins (16.00).
b) E.g. 13.00-14.00.
c) 10.15 to 16.30 = 6 hours and 15 mins, so they will need to pay £8.00.

Q2 a) The group need to be there for 10.30, so they need to set off 40 mins before, which is 9.50.
b) £56 ÷ 8 = £7 each.
c) Each friend needs to pay £28 for their own place, £7 for the minibus, and £28 ÷ 7 = £4 for their share of Liam's place on the course.
In total: £28 + £7 + £4 = £39.

Page 17
Q3 a) £16.50 ÷ £3.50 = 4.7142... rides, so they would need to go on at least 5 rides each to make it worth buying the pass.
b) They only need to pay for 3 passes with the offer, so it will cost in total 3 × £16.50 = £49.50.
The boys each owe Wayne £49.50 ÷ 4 = £12.38.
c) Wayne should have £20 − £6 = £14 to spend on photos.
4 × £3.20 = £12.80, so he will have enough for the four photos.

Q4 a) It took a quarter of a tank of fuel to get there, so it should take half a tank for the full journey.
Total cost of fuel and parking = (£45 ÷ 2) + £5 = £27.50.
Each person owes £27.50 ÷ 4 = £6.88.
b) Time = Distance ÷ Speed
= 35 miles ÷ 70 mph
= 0.5 hours = 30 mins. If they set off at 6.15 pm they should arrive back at 6.45 pm.

Page 18
Q5 a) Distance = Speed × Time
= 10 mph × 3 hours = 30 miles.
b) Cycle route seeing all the sights
= 9 + 5 + 3 + 1 + 15 = 33 miles, which is too far.
Cycle route seeing the castle, Roman ruins and lake = 11 + 3 + 1 + 15 = 30 miles:

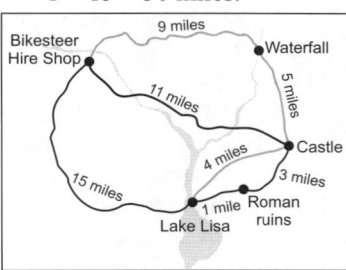

Q6 a) The girls need to see the 11.30-13.30 film showing, because the later one will not finish in time for the Quick Flash Sale at 15.30. This means they need to see the 10.00-11.00 fashion show, so that they can walk to the cinema by 11.30.
b) The film finishes at 13.30, and they need to set off for Bedhams for the sale 20 mins before 15.30 = 15.10. This leaves them 15.10 − 13.30 = 1 h 40 mins for bowling and lunch. Bowling lasts for an hour, so they have 40 mins for lunch.

Page 19
Q7 For single boat trips it would cost £3.75 + £2.20 + £4.50 = £10.45, or for two returns £7 + £4 = £11, so this is not as cheap as the hop on/hop off ticket at £10.
Hop on/hop off + museum entry = £10 + £4.50 + £5.90 = £20.40.
The Super Saver gives 20% off museum entry. Full price = £4.50 + £5.90 = £10.40.
With discount:
£10.40 − (20 ÷ 100 × £10.40) = £8.32.
Total cost with Super Saver = £8.32 + £13.50 = £21.82.
So the lowest amount is £20.40 with the hop on/hop off ticket.

Answers (Foundation Level): P.20 — P.23

Q8 If C is the cost, and T is the time, then the cost for the kayaks is:
C = 3 + 12T. C can be no more than £30, so 30 = 3 + 12T.
T = (30 − 3) ÷ 12 = 2.25, so they would have 2 full hours in the kayaks.
The cost of the sailboat is:
C = (3 × 3) + 25T
C = 9 + 25T. C can be no more than 3 × £30 = £90, so
90 = 9 + 25T
T = (90 − 9) ÷ 25 = 3.24, so they would have 3 full hours in the sailboat. So the sailboat gives them the longest time on the lake.

Shopping
Page 20
Q1 a) £30 − £20.25 = £9.75 so yes, she got the correct amount of change.
b) £3.80 ÷ 2 = £1.90.
So one plus one at half price = £3.80 + £1.90 = £5.70.
c) £2.20 + £0.45 + £0.60 = £3.25, so she has been overcharged by 25p.
d) Emma has been overcharged £1.90 for the chicken and 25p for the meal deal. £1.90 + £0.25 = £2.15, so the cashier hasn't refunded her the correct amount — she needs to give her an extra 10p.

Q2 a) MooveeWorld:
£11.99 × 3 = £35.97
(plus free P&P).
Films4everyone:
£30 + £4.50 = £34.50.
So it's cheaper for John to get the DVDs from Films4everyone.
b) MooveeWorld:
£11.99 × 5 = £59.95.
Films4everyone:
£30 + (2 × £12.99) = £55.98 + £4.50 = £60.48.
So it's cheaper for John to get the 5 DVDs from MooveeWorld.

Page 21
Q3 a) 2 × 11 = 22 orange quarters for each team.
b) 22 for each team = 44 orange quarters. 44 ÷ 4 = 11 oranges in total.
c) 500 ml × 11 = 5500 ml = 5.5 l, so Lynn needs to buy 6 litre bottles.

Q4 a) Between them, the 2 dogs eat 1.5 tins a day. 1.5 × 7 days = 10.5, so Jenny would need to buy 11 tins.
b) 10 kg = 10 000 g.
Between them, the 2 dogs eat 250 g twice a day = 500 g.
10 000 ÷ 500 = 20, so the 10 kg bag will last the dogs 20 days.
c) 10.5 tins for one week, so 10.5 × 2 = 21 tins for 2 weeks. One 10 kg bag will last for 20 days, which is enough for 2 weeks (14 days). So Pete should buy 21 tins and 1 bag.
d) Tins: 21 × £1.24 = £26.04.
Bags: 1 × £25.80 = £25.80.
So Jenny owes Pete £26.04 + £25.80 = £51.84.

Page 22
Q5 2 hours = 120 min
Economy tariff:
100 inclusive min + 20 min charged at 15p/min =
20 × 15 = 300p = £3.
50 inclusive texts + 50 texts charged at 10p/message =
50 × 10 = 500p = £5
Unlimited data = £5.50
Total = £10.99 + £3 + £5 + £5.50 = £24.49.
Standard tariff:
unlimited data = £5.50
so total = £17.99 + £5.50 = £23.49.
Roamer tariff = £23.99 with no additional charges, so the cheapest option for Mel is the Standard Tariff.

Q6 a) The shoes will have 5% off if she buys them today.
5 ÷ 100 × £70 = £3.50 off, so they will cost £70 − £3.50 = £66.50.
With her friend's money, Alison has £48 + £15 = £63 so no, she won't have enough money.
b) The shoes will have 10% off if Alison buys them on the store card. 10 ÷ 100 × £70 = £7 off, so they will cost £70 − £7 = £63. She will have to pay 3% interest on the £63.
3 ÷ 100 × £63 = £1.89, so in total she will pay £63 + £1.89 = £64.89 for the shoes.

Page 23
Q7 Whitey Whites: 125 g per wash; 1.5 kg = 1500 g.
1500 ÷ 125 = 12 washes.
£5.10 ÷ 12 = 42.5p per wash.
Soapy Suds: 2 kg = 2000 g;
125 g per wash.
2000 ÷ 125 = 16 washes.
£6.28 ÷ 16 = 39.25p per wash.
Eco-wash: 28 ÷ 2 = 14 washes.
£6.30 ÷ 14 = 45p per wash.
Soapy Suds costs the least per wash, so it is the best value for money.

Q8 He needs a carpet 5 m × 4 m = 20 m^2.
LastStock: £160.
UniPrice: £7.99 × 20 = £159.80.
Carpet Discounts: 50% off RRP.
50 ÷ 100 × £19.50 = £9.75 off, so price = £9.75 per m^2.
With another 20% off:
20 ÷ 100 × £9.75 = £1.95 off.
£9.75 − £1.95 = £7.80 per m^2.
£7.80 × 20 = £156.
So Carpet Discounts would give Syed the best deal.

Answers (Foundation Level)

Answers (Foundation Level): P.24 — P.27

Jobs
Page 24
Q1 a) Biologist:
(£30 000 + £28 000 + £32 000) ÷ 3 = £30 000.
Chemist:
(£34 000 + £52 000 + £25 000) ÷ 3 = £37 000.
Physicist:
(£48 000 + £28 000 + £30 000) ÷ 3 = £35 333.
So the Chemist has the highest average salary.
b) Biologist:
£32 000 − £28 000 = £4000.
Chemist:
£52 000 − £25 000 = £27 000.
Physicist:
£48 000 − £28 000 = £20 000.
So the Biologist has the smallest range of salaries.
c) Average science salary =
(£30 000 + £28 000 + £32 000 + £34 000 + £52 000 + £25 000 + £48 000 + £28 000 + £30 000) ÷ 9 = £34 100 to the nearest £100.

Q2 a) Ben works 2 days per week and Charlie works 2 days per week. Andrea works 7 − (2 + 2) = 3 days per week. So Andrea, Ben and Charlie should split their wages into the ratio 3 : 2 : 2.
b) Total parts in ratio = 7. Each part = £56 ÷ 7 = £8. Andrea should get 3 × £8 = £24.
Ben and Charlie should each get 2 × £8 = £16 per week.
c) Charlie worked 2 days so they'll work 1 extra day each. Andrea will work 4 days so will earn 4 × £8 = £32 per week. Ben will work 3 days = 4 × £8 = £24 per week.

Page 25
Q3 a) Josh works 4 hours a day, 3 times a week = 12 hours a week.
12 × £5.50 = £66 per week.
b) He spends £20 a week so he saves £66 − £20 = £46 per week.
The deposit is £100 so 100 ÷ 46 = 2.173... so he needs to work for 3 weeks to save up £100 for the deposit.
c) The holiday costs £306 in total. £306 ÷ 6 weeks = £51, so he needs to save £51 per week.

Q4 a) Manor hire cost = £2500 for 5 days. Chef costs £250 × 5 = £1250. Cleaner costs £60.
Total cost = £2500 + £1250 + £60 = £3810. For a group of 20, she will need to charge £3810 ÷ 20 = £190.50 per person to cover her costs.
b) £240 × 20 = £4800 − £3810 = £990 profit.
c) 14 × £240 = £3360, which doesn't cover the running costs of £3810 so no, it's not worth Polly running it for only 14 people as she would lose money.

Page 26
Q5 a) £350 ÷ £15 = 23.3333... so she needs at least 24 lessons per week to keep her earnings the same.
b) Total number of lessons in 4 weeks = 4 × 25.25 = 101, so she earned £15 × 101 = £1515. In her previous job she would have earned £350 × 4 = £1400, so she has earned an extra £1515 − £1400 = £115.
c) At 25.25 lessons per week for 52 − 4 = 48 weeks, she would teach 25.25 × 48 = 1212 lessons per year. She needs to charge £26 000 ÷ 1212 = £21.45 per lesson = £21.50 to the nearest 50p.

Q6 a) No tax paid on the first £6475. Danni will pay 20% tax on (£16 000 − £6475) = £9525. £9525 × 20 ÷ 100 = £1905 per year. Each month she will have £1905 ÷ 12 = £158.75 tax deducted.
b) Monthly salary = £16 000 ÷ 12 = £1333.33. So she will have: £1333.33 − (£158.75 + £350 + £150 + £200) = £474.58 left.

Page 27
Q7 Current wage + 5% pay rise: £250 + (£250 × 5 ÷ 100) = £262.50 per week.
New job: £300 per week. Weekly difference = £300 − £262.50 = £37.50. Course costs £1600, so it will take £1600 ÷ £37.50 = 42.7 weeks to pay off. There are 26 weeks in 6 months, so it will take longer than 6 months to pay it off.

Q8 £12 000 + 13% of sales over £5000. Target sales are £7600, so she gets 13% of (£7600 − £5000) = £2600. £2600 × 13 ÷ 100 = £338 a month. £338 × 12 = £4056 a year.
Total annual earnings = £4065 + £12 000 = £16 056.

Answers (Foundation Level): P.28 — P.32

Going Out

Page 28

Q1 a) Dee should arrive 5 mins + 25 mins = 30 mins after 20.15, which is 20.45.
b) Stef needs to leave by 10 mins before 20.45, which is 20.35.

Q2 The drinks will cost £3.15 + £3.40 + £3.40 = £9.95, so £10 will be enough.

Q3 a) 10% of £24 = £24 × 0.10 = £2.40, so total = £24 + £2.40 = £26.40.
b) £26.40 split between 3 girls = £26.40 ÷ 3 = £8.80 each.

Page 29

Q4 a) 6 slices of pizza each is 24 slices in total. This means ordering either 4 small, 3 medium or 2 large pizzas.
4 small pizzas cost 4 × £5.50 = £22.
3 medium pizzas cost 3 × £7.50 = £22.50.
2 large pizzas cost 2 × £9.50 = £19.
So it is cheapest to buy large. Cheapest drink is cordial at £0.40 each, so lowest total amount = £19 + (4 × £0.40) = £20.60.
b) The boys would need to order two lots of Meal Deal 1, so this would cost 2 × £10 = £20. It is cheaper to order Meal Deal 2 plus four of the cheapest drinks. This would cost £18 + (4 × £0.40) = £19.60.

Q5 a) 20% of £37.40 = 20 ÷ 100 × £37.40 = £7.48.
So total amount = £37.40 + £7.48 = £44.88 = £44.90 to the nearest 10p.
b) The three other boys need to split £44.90 − £10 = £34.90 between 3.
£34.90 ÷ 3 = £11.63 = £11.60 to the nearest 10p.

Page 30

Q6 a) The latest bus Hannah can get from Hastwick leaves at 1705.
b) The bus leaves Nauton Green at 1735, so Wayne needs to set off by 10 mins before this, which is 1725.
c) The film plus trailers will last 20 mins + 168 mins = 188 mins, or 3 hrs and 8 mins. Starting at 1800, it should finish at 2108. The last bus leaves Minsterbury High St. at 2125, so they should be in time to catch it.

Q7 a) 330 ml ÷ 100p = 3.3 ml per penny.
500 ml ÷ 200p = 2.5 ml per penny.
So the 330 ml can is better value for money.
b) 50 g ÷ 130p = 0.38 g per penny.
75 g ÷ 225p = 0.33 g per penny.
150 g ÷ 450p = 0.33 g per penny.
So the small 50 g bag is the best value for money.

Page 31

Q8 The cheapest seats are in the Circle. Buying individual tickets would cost:
Adults: 4 × £30 = £120
OAPs: 2 × £25 = £50
Students: 3 × £25 = £75
Children: 1 × £15 = £15
Total = £120 + £50 + £75 + £15 = £260. They would get 15% off as they are a group of 10.
15% of £260 = 15 ÷ 100 × 260 = £39.
Total with discount = £260 − £39 = £221.
Alternatively, they could buy 2 'Group of 5' tickets at 2 × £135 = £270.
15% of £270 = 15 ÷ 100 × 270 = £40.50, so total with discount = £270 − £40.50 = £229.50.
So the lowest total price = £221.

Q9 a) E.g. total cost C is:
£2.50 × no. of ice cream tubs (T) + £1.50 × no. of drinks (D),
so: $C = 2.5T + 1.5D$.
He must buy 10 drinks, so D = 10, and so
$C = 2.5T + (1.5 × 10)$,
$C = 2.5T + 15$.
b) The total cost can be no more than £20, so C =
20 = 2.5T + 15.
20 − 15 = 2.5T
5 = 2.5T
T = 5 ÷ 2.5 = 2, so he can only afford to buy 2 tubs of ice cream.

Decorating

Page 32

Q1 a) To the nearest 10 mm, 615 mm is the smallest the gap could be.
b) The widths are rounded to the nearest mm, so they could all be up to 0.5 mm bigger. Maximum widths are:
A — 620.5 mm,
B — 614.5 mm,
C — 615.5 mm.
c) The only oven that will definitely fit the gap is oven B, as its maximum width is smaller than the minimum width of the gap.

Q2 a) Area = 75 cm × 50 cm = 3750 cm^2.
b) Donna should expect to pay: 3750 cm^2 ÷ 100 cm^2 × £1 = £37.50.

Page 33

Q3 a) Vin will need 0.15 × 40 m^2 = 6 litres of paint.
b) Total number of parts in the ratio = 1 + 2 = 3. Each part is 6 litres ÷ 3 = 2 litres of paint. Vin needs 2 parts white paint which is 2 × 2 litres = 4 litres white.
c) Vin needs 1 part blue paint = 2 litres, so he will need 2 tins of blue paint.

Answers (Foundation Level): P.34 — P.37

Q4 a) E.g.

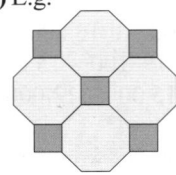

b) Area of square tiles =
5 cm × 5 cm × 20 tiles =
500 cm².
Area of octagonal tiles =
120.7 cm × 20 = 2414 cm².
Total = 500 + 2414 = 2914 cm².

c) Wall is 1 m long = 100 cm,
and 0.5 m high = 50 cm.
Area of wall = 50 cm × 100 cm
= 5000 cm². Total area of the
tiles is only 2914 cm², so there
is not enough to cover the area
of wall.

Page 34

Q5 a) Perimeter of room =
4.7 + 5.1 + 2.3 + 1.1 + 2.4 +
4.0 = 19.6 m.
Length of rail needed =
Perimeter of room − Widths of
doors and windows =
19.6 − (1.2 + 1.2 + 1.1) = 16.1 m.

b) Teresa would need 16.1 ÷ 0.7 =
23 lengths of Wood A, costing
23 × £0.75 = £17.25.
She would need 17 lengths of
Wood B, costing 17 × £0.95 =
£16.15. So the least amount
she could spend is £16.15.

Q6 a) Area of flooring needed =
(4.7 m × 4.0 m) +
(2.3 m × 1.1 m) =
18.8 m² + 2.53 m² = 21.33 m².

b) There is a difference in price of
£8 − £5 = £3 per square metre.
Teresa would save
£3 × 21.33 m² = £63.99 by
choosing laminate flooring.

Page 35

Q7 As there's no pattern on the paper
which needs to be matched up,
Hayley can fit exact numbers of
the 0.5 m widths of paper across
the widths of the walls, and also
either side of the door and window.
Window width =
6 m − (2 m + 2 m) = 2 m
Window height =
3 m − (0.5 m + 1 m) = 1.5 m
Door width =
5 m − (3 m + 1 m) = 1 m
Door height = 3 m − 1 m = 2 m.
So, total area to be papered =
(2 × 5 m × 3 m) + (2 × 6 m × 3 m)
− (2 m × 1.5 m) − (1 m × 2 m)
= 61 m².
Each roll of paper contains
10 m × 0.5 m = 5 m².
61 m² ÷ 5 m² = 12.2, so Hayley
will need to buy at least 13 rolls.
She also needs a packet of paste
for every 4 rolls. 13 ÷ 4 = 3.25,
so she will need at least 4 packets
of paste.

Q8 a) Area of walls to be painted =
(2 × 5 m × 3 m) +
(2 × 4 m × 3 m) − (2 m × 1 m)
− (1 m × 2 m) = 50 m².
Hayley will need 0.15 × 50 m²
= 7.5 litres of paint. Each tin is
2 litres, so she will need 4 tins.
Length of border needed
= 5 + 4 + 5 + 4 − 2 − 1 = 15 m.
15 m ÷ 6 m per roll = 2.5,
so she will need 3 rolls of
border.

b) Paint ≈ £9 × 4 tins = £36.
Border ≈ £5 × 3 rolls = £15.
Paste (1 pack for 3 rolls) ≈ £1.
Roller and Tray ≈ £5.
Brush Set ≈ £3.
Total = £36 + £15 + £1 + £5 +
£3 = £60.

Gardening
Page 36

Q1 a) Perimeter = 2 + 3 + 2 + 3 = 10 m.

b) Aftab will need 10 m ÷ 0.5 m =
20 border lengths.

c) Across the width Aftab will
need 3 m ÷ 0.5 m = 6 slabs.
Across the length he will need
2 m ÷ 0.5 m = 4 slabs. So he
needs to buy 6 × 4 = 24 slabs.

Q2 a) The possible arrangements are:

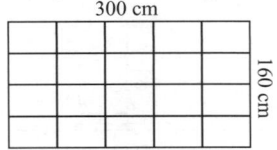

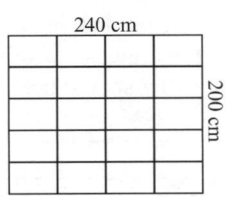

b) Perimeter of top arrangement
= 300 + 160 + 300 + 160 =
920 cm. Perimeter of bottom
arrangement = 240 + 200 + 240
+ 200 = 880 cm.
The bottom arrangement has
the smallest perimeter, so
the smallest length of border
required is 880 cm = 8.8 m.

Page 37

Q3 a) Helena's lawn is roughly
triangular, with area =
½ × 10 m × 8 m = 40 m².

b) Helena needs 0.5 litres × 40 m²
= 20 litres of diluted treatment.

c) Total number of parts in ratio
= 1 + 9 = 10 parts. Each part is
20 litres ÷ 10 = 2 litres. Helena
needs 1 part = 2 litres of the
undiluted treatment.

Q4 a) Area of lawn =
(5 m × 9 m) + (7 m × 5 m)
= 45 m² + 35 m² = 80 m².
Area of one roll of turf =
1 m × 5 m = 5 m². So Jordan
needs to order 80 m² ÷ 5 m² =
16 rolls of turf.

b) Price of order ≈
(15 rolls × £5 per roll) + £15
delivery = £75 + £15 = £90.

Answers (Foundation Level): P.38 — P.41

Page 38
Q5 a) and b):

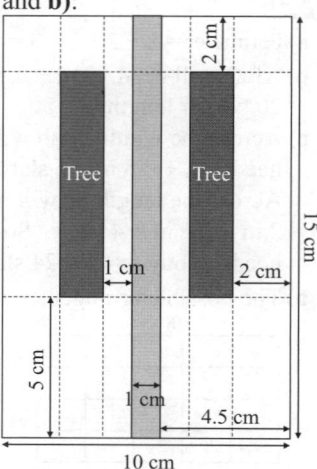

Dimensions on drawing refer to what the dimensions of the scale drawing should be.

Q6 a)

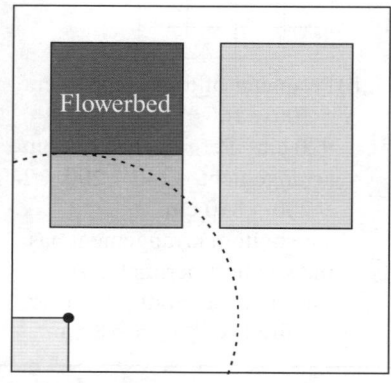

b) From the scale plan, flowerbed is 3.5 m wide and 3 m long. So Cathy would need 3.5 + 3 + 3.5 + 3 = 13 m of border.

Page 39
Q7 Circumference of pond = π × 2 m = 6.2831... m = 628.3185... cm. Number of tiles required = 628.3185... cm ÷ 10 cm = 62.8318... There are 10 tiles per box, so Harry will need 7 boxes.

Q8 Radius of pond = 2 m ÷ 2 = 1 m. Volume of pond = (π × 1^2) × 1 m = 3.14 m^3. 3.14 m^3 × 2 fish per m^3 = 6.28 fish, so Harry can have a maximum of 6 fish in his pond.

City Planning
Page 40
Q1 a) Glass on outer walls = perimeter.
A = 9 + 4 + 3 + 3 + 3 + 3 + 3 + 4 = 32 m.
B = 7 + 7 + 2 + 2 + 2 + 2 + 3 + 7 = 32 m.
C = 7 + 6 + 2 + 1 + 3 + 1 + 2 + 6 = 28 m.
So Design C uses the least amount of glass.

b) Area of glass needed for Design C = perimeter × height = 28 m × 3 m × 6 floors = 504 m^2. Glass is £25 per m^2, so cost = £25 × 504 = £12 600.

Q2 a) Measurements refer to what they should be on scale drawings.
Front Elevation:

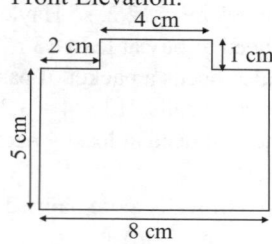

Side Elevation:

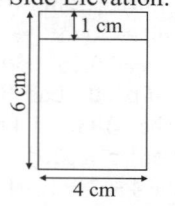

Plan:

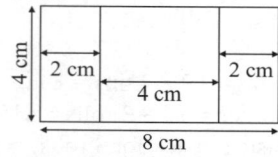

b) Area of front of building = (80 m × 50 m) + (40 m × 10 m) = 4000 m^2 + 400 m^2 = 4400 m^2. So 4400 panes of glass with area 1 m^2 will be needed.

Page 41
Q3 a) 80% reduction of 15 000 vehicles: 80 ÷ 100 × 15 000 = 12 000. 15 000 − 12 000 = 3000.
So 3000 vehicles would pass through Sheepston each day.

b) 12 000 vehicles would use the bypass in one day, so 12 000 × £3 = £36 000.

c) £36 000 × 365 = £13 140 000 in one year.
The bypass cost £35 million, 35 000 000 ÷ 13 140 000 = 2.66... So it would take approx. 3 years for the toll charge to pay for the building of the bypass.

Q4 a) Total number of vehicles in one week = 10 261 + 8895 + 908 = 20 064. Average per day = 20 064 ÷ 7 = 2866 vehicles (to the nearest whole).

b) 80% of 15 000 vehicles = 80 ÷ 100 × 15 000 = 12 000. If the target has been met, there should be no more than 15 000 − 12 000 = 3000 vehicles per day. The survey shows there are only 2866 per day, so yes, the target has been met.

c) E.g. the survey could have been done over a longer period of time than just one week / the survey could have been repeated at different weeks during the year.

Page 42
Q5 a) 10 800 new houses built in total, 10 800 ÷ 360 = 30, so 1° represents 30 new houses. 'Low cost' = less than £150 000, so need to measure the '£0-£99 999' and '£100 000-£149 999' segments on the chart. These measure 60°, and so represent 60° × 30 houses = 1800 new houses.
1800 ÷ 10 800 × 100 = 16.7%. Their target is '1 in 5', which is 1 ÷ 5 × 100 = 20%, so no, the committee are not on target.

Answers (Foundation Level): P.43 — P.47

b) Total number of houses =
10 800 + 1500 = 12 300. 20%
of new houses should be 'low
cost'.
20% of 12 300 =
20 ÷ 100 × 12 300 = 2460 low
cost houses. 1800 have already
been built, so 2460 – 1800 =
660 of the new houses need to
be 'low cost'.

Q6 a) The table shows that every
5 years the population increases
by 1800, so in 2015 the
population should be:
46 600 + 1800 = 48 400.
b) E.g.
Population increases by 1800
every 5 years. From 2010 to
2060 is 50 years = 10 × 5 years.
10 × 1800 = 18 000, so
population in 2060 will be
46 600 + 18 000 = 64 600.

Page 43
Q7 a) 5 × 15 cm = 75 cm.
b)

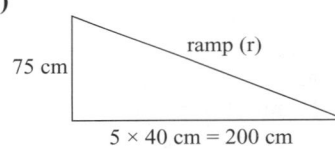

Using Pythagoras:
$r^2 = 75^2 + 200^2$
$r^2 = 5625 + 40\,000 = 45\,625$
$r = 213.6... = 214$ cm, so the
ramp needs to be 214 cm long.

Q8 Car park = 10 m × 25 m = 250 m^2,
so the tarmac will cost 250 × 45
= £11 250. 5% discount because
it's over £10 000, so
5 ÷ 100 × 11 250 = £562.50.
£11 250 – £562.50 = £10 687.50
for the tarmac.
Plus delivery charge =
£10 687.50 + 56 = £10 743.50.
Plus labour cost for 4 hours
= £10 743.50 + (4 × 65)
= £11 003.50.
So it will cost £11 003.50 in
total to resurface the car park.

Paying Bills
Page 44
Q1 a) 195.62 + 102.48 + 85.80 +
156.22 = £540.12.
b) 540.12 ÷ 12 = £45.01.
c) 5 ÷ 100 × 45.01 = £2.25
£45.01 – £2.25 = £42.76.

Q2 Cost = £12 000 – £3500 = £8500.
Save up to £610 a year:
£8500 ÷ £610 = 13.9344... years
so it will take him at least
14 years to recover the cost.

Page 45
Q3 a) Average usage =
54 m^3 a year ÷ 12 = 4.5 m^3
a month. From the graph,
4.5 m^3 a month = £11 × 12
= £132 a year.
b) Showing the fixed rate on the
graph, £198 ÷ 12 = £16.50 a
month:

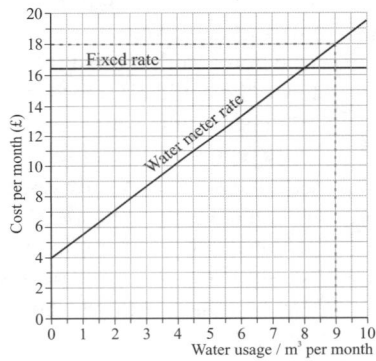

Tim should switch back to the
fixed water rate if they use
anything over 8 m^3 a month.
If Tim's girlfriend also uses an
average amount of water then
they will use 2 × 4.5 m^3 = 9 m^3
a month, so it would be cheaper
to switch back to the fixed rate.

Q4 325 units @ 16p = £52.
Remaining units = (478 – 325)
= 153 units @ 11p = 153 × 0.11
= £16.83.
£16.83 + £52 = £68.83.
VAT is 5% of £68.83
= 5 ÷ 100 × £68.83 = £3.44,
so total = £68.83 + £3.44 =
£72.27.
Anna's bill is £76.20 so she has
been overcharged by
(76.20 – 72.27) = £3.93.

Page 46
Q5 a) 50 × £12.99 = £649.50 should
have been charged for the
buffet. £779.40 – £649.50
= £129.90, so she has been
overcharged by £129.90.
b) £250 + £649.50 = £899.50.
17.5% VAT =
17.5 ÷ 100 × £899.50 =
£157.41.
Total cost = £899.50 + £157.41
= £1056.91.
Minus deposit:
£1056.91 – £200 = £856.91.
Pay half this amount:
£856.91 ÷ 2 =
£428.46 by 1st May.

Q6 (5.99 × 3) + (12.99 × 15) =
17.97 + 194.85 = £212.82 over
18 months. This is
£212.82 ÷ 18 = £11.8233... per
month. One quarter is 3 months,
so £11.8233... × 3 = £35.47 per
quarter. So yes, he is on the
correct contract.

Page 47
Q7 Average use: 90 minutes call time;
216 text messages.
TextyText:
extra 60 mins @ 17p/min
= 60 × 17 = 1020p = £10.20.
£10.20 + £12.76 = £22.96.
17.5% VAT = 17.5 ÷ 100 × £22.96
= £4.02.
Total = £22.96 + £4.02 = £26.98.
TextyTalk:
extra 66 texts @ 9p/msg
= 66 × 9 = 594p = £5.94.
£5.94 + £16.16 = £22.10.
17.5% VAT = 17.5 ÷ 100 × £22.10
= £3.87.
Total = £22.10 + £3.87 = £25.97.
TextyTalkPlus:
extra 16 texts @ 9p/msg
= 16 × 9 = 144p = £1.44.
£1.44 + £17.86 = £19.30.
17.5% VAT = 17.5 ÷ 100 × £19.30
= £3.38.
Total = £19.30 + £3.38 = £22.68.
So Jane should be on the
TextyTalkPlus tariff to reduce her
bill to under £25.

Answers (Foundation Level): P.48 — P.50

Q8 Repair cost = 195 + 75 + 85 + 210 + 35 + 95 = £695.
17.5% VAT = 17.5 ÷ 100 × 695 = £121.63.
£695 + £121.63 = £816.63.
Car's value drops 10% each year for two years.
<u>Value in 2009</u>: 10% of £995 = 10 ÷ 100 × £995 = £99.50.
£995 – £99.50 = £895.50.
<u>Value in 2010</u>: 10% of £895.50 = 10 ÷ 100 × £895.50 = £89.55.
£895.50 – £89.55 = £805.95.
So yes, she paid more to fix her car than it car was worth in 2010.

In the News
Page 48
Q1 a) $\frac{3}{4}$ of the pie chart represents people who said MDobz were the best. As a percentage, $\frac{3}{4}$ of 100% = 75%.
  b) 20 people voted in total, so $\frac{3}{4}$ × 20 = 15 people.
  c) Any two reasons from e.g. there are not enough people in the sample / the question is leading / they have only asked people who read their website so are likely to agree with their opinions / the answers to choose from are not clear.

Q2 a) In order of price:
Trundle properties:
£90 000, £95 000, £98 000, £100 000, £110 000, £115 000, £120 000, £122 000, £130 000, £345 000. There are 10 prices, so the median is between the 5th (£110 000) and the 6th (£115 000) =
(£110 000 + £115 000) ÷ 2 = £112 500.
Udderston properties:
£54 000, £60 000, £75 000, £95 000, £120 000, £125 000, £155 000, £160 000, £165 000, £290 000. There are 10 prices, so the median is between the 5th (£120 000) and the 6th (£125 000) =
(£120 000 + £125 000) ÷ 2 = £122 500.
So Udderston has the highest median house price.

  b) Mean house price is the sum of the prices ÷ 10.
Trundle mean =
£1 325 000 ÷ 10 = £132 500.
Udderston mean =
£1 299 000 ÷ 10 = £129 900.
So Trundle has the highest mean house price.
  c) There is one property in Trundle worth £345 000 which is a lot higher than the other values. This could affect the mean but not the median, so the median will be more reliable.

Page 49
Q3 a) Any 2 from e.g. he could stand somewhere other than the job centre as there are likely to be a high number of unemployed people near the job centre / he could do the survey at a weekend when there is a fairer mix of people who work and who don't work around the town / he could ask more than 10 to get results which are more representative of the population of the whole town / he could ask them in a less personal way as unemployment is a sensitive issue, and people may be reluctant to give honest answers.
  b) The graphs only show that Localville had a higher proportion of people unemployed than Big City. As there are likely to be more people in the city, this means there won't necessarily be more people unemployed in Localville, as the bigger proportion is of a smaller number of people overall.

Q4 a) The scale on the bar chart does not start at zero, so it looks like there are 5 times more giant toads than normal toads from the sizes of the bars. Using the actual values, 20 ÷ 15 = 1.25, so there are only 1.25 times the amount of giant toads as normal toads.
  b) Total number of toads in park = 16 + 20 = 36. Angle for normal toads = (16 ÷ 36) × 360° = 160°:

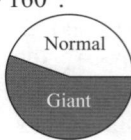

Page 50
Q5 a) 'Eyes' has won 7 times in his last 10 games, so his probability of winning is $\frac{7}{10}$ = 0.7 = 70%.
  b) Mean stare time is the total over all the games ÷ no. of games.
'Eyes' mean = 445 mins ÷ 10 = 44.5 mins.
Arthur's mean = 285 mins ÷ 5 = 57 mins,
so Arthur would be the winner with the highest mean stare time.

Q6 Using the mean (total goal difference ÷ 20) as the average:
Nutters Utd:
Mean = 15 ÷ 20 = 0.75.
Headly Town:
Mean = 19 ÷ 20 = 0.95
Noggin City:
Mean = 10 ÷ 20 = 0.5.
So Headly Town have the highest average goal difference.
Using the range to measure consistency:
Nutters Utd: Range = +6 − -3 = 9.
Headly Town: Range = +9 − -7 = 16
Noggin City: Range = +3− -2 = 5.
Noggin City have the smallest range, which means they have the most consistent results.

Answers (Foundation Level): P.51 — P.54

Health and Fitness
Page 51
Q1 a) E.g. she could include a stamped addressed envelope for them to return it / offer an incentive to return it, such as enter people into a prize draw.
b) E.g. the questions are too open-ended so members could give many different responses to each one.
c) Jane would get more useful responses by including option boxes for members to tick with a choice of suitable responses, e.g. for question 1 the responses could be the number of times per month they visit the gym, with appropriate number ranges.
d) E.g. phone or email people instead / ask members as they come to the centre / do secondary research to see which leisure centres are successful and what facilities they offer.

Q2 a) Ribble Rovers have $(12 \times 3 \text{ pts}) + (2 \times 1 \text{ pt})$ = 38 pts.
Duddon Dragons have $(13 \times 3 \text{ pts}) + (2 \times 1 \text{ pt})$ = 41 pts.
b) A win for Ribble Rovers gives them another 3 points, leaving them on 38 + 3 = 41 points, the same as Duddon Dragons. The score of 4-2 will leave Ribble Rovers with a goal difference of 9 + (4 − 2) = +11, and Duddon Dragons with a goal difference of 10 + (2 − 4) = +8, which is lower than Ribble Rovers. So yes, it is enough for Ribble Rovers to win the league.

Page 52
Q3 a)

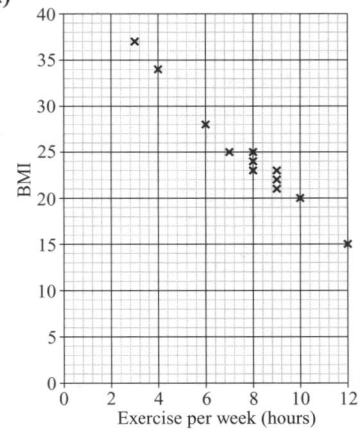

b) There is a negative correlation, so the more they exercise per week, the lower their BMI.
c) Jane's claim could be incorrect because there could be other factors involved which affect the BMI, e.g. diet. Also, we don't know the BMI of people before they joined Local Leisure Ltd, so there is nothing to compare it to.

Q4 a) Mean = (2700 + 2550 + 2450 + 2650 + 2500 + 2750 + 2950) ÷ 7 = 2650 calories per day.
b) In one week, Clive will have consumed (2650 − 2500) × 7 = 1050 excess calories. This will take 1050 cals ÷ 25 cals per min = 42 mins to burn off. 42 mins ÷ 25 mins per session = 1.68, so he needs 2 sessions per week.

Page 53
Q5 a) Speed = Distance ÷ Time
Average speed for the first 5 km run in 26 mins:
= 5 km ÷ 26 mins =
0.19 km/min.
Average speed for the second 5 km run in 32 mins:
Speed = Distance ÷ Time
= 5 km ÷ 32 mins =
0.16 km/min.
So Steve's average speed was higher in the first half of the race.
b) The graph has a steep gradient at the end (the last km), which shows he was running faster.
c) Time = Distance ÷ Speed.
Speed = 10 km ÷ 12 km/h = 0.8333... hours.
0.8333... × 60 mins = 50 mins.

Q6 a) Mean number of runs = total over 5 matches ÷ 5.
Mark: 244 ÷ 5 = 48.8.
Ryan: 254 ÷ 5 = 50.8.
Peter: 235 ÷ 5 = 47.0.
Geoff: 251 ÷ 5 = 50.2.
So Fred should select Ryan, with a batting average of 50.8.
b) Most consistent player is the one with the smallest range of runs.
Mark: 61 − 38 = 23.
Ryan: 58 − 42 = 16.
Peter: 72 − 22 = 50.
Geoff: 57 − 43 = 14.
So Geoff has the most consistent batting score.
c) Without match 5, Peter's mean score = (72 + 41 + 49 + 51) ÷ 4 = 53.25, which is the best batting average, so yes, this will affect Fred's selection decision.

Page 54
Q7 PAYG swim:
£3 per swim × 2 swims per week × 52 weeks = £312.
PAYG gym:
£3.50 per week × 52 weeks = £182.
Swim membership =
£25 per month × 12 months = £300.
Gym membership =
£35 per month × 12 months = £420.
Combined membership =
£45 per month × 12 months = £540.
Cheapest combination =
Swim membership + PAYG gym pass = £300 + £182 = £482 for one year.

Answers (Foundation Level): P.55 — P.58

Q8 The three time sections will each take 10 mins. In the first 10 mins, 1.75 miles were covered in the race. Speed = Distance ÷ Time = (1.75 miles ÷ 10 mins) × 60 mins = 10.5 mph.
In the second 10 mins, (2.5 − 1.75) = 0.75 miles were covered in the race. Speed = (0.75 miles ÷ 10 mins) × 60 = 4.5 mph.
In the third 10 mins, (4 − 2.5) = 1.5 miles were covered in the race. Speed = (1.5 miles ÷ 10 mins) × 60 = 9 mph.

Car Boot Sale
Page 55
Q1 a) 0.80 + 0.80 + 1.20 + 2.50 = £5.30.
b) Cost of a book and a teddy bear is 0.80 + 1.30 = £2.10. 10 − 2.10 = £7.90, so Sarah should give £7.90 change.
c) Sarah started the day with £21.70 so she has made 87.50 − 21.70 = £65.80.

Q2 a) Jonny has 3 of the 12 books so needs to buy 9 books. Each book is £0.75 so this will cost him 0.75 × 9 = £6.75. So it's cheaper for him to buy the whole set.
b) Jonny has £8, he's spent £6 on books so has 8 − 6 = £2 left. Marbles cost £0.45 each. 2 ÷ 0.45 = 4.44... so he can buy 4 marbles.

Page 56
Q3 a) Price of 3 cushions at stall 151: 2 cushions cost £2.80 each and the third cushion is free, so 2.80 × 2 = £5.60.
Price of 3 cushions at stall 210: 2 cushions cost £2.40 each and the third one is half price, so (2.40 × 2) + 1.20 = £6.
So Dave should buy the cushions from stall 151.

b) Price of 4 cushions at stall 151: 3 cushions cost £2.80 each and one cushion is free, so 2.80 × 3 = £8.40.
Price of 4 cushions at stall 210: 2 cushions cost £2.40 each and 2 cushions are half price, so (2.40 × 2) + (1.20 × 2) = £7.20.
So Dave should buy the cushions from stall 210.
c) Dave is owed 20 − 7.20 = £12.80 change, so no, he has not been given the right amount.

Q4 a) Set of computer games:
15 ÷ 100 × 3.5 = 0.525
3.5 − 0.525 = £2.98
Video player:
15 ÷ 100 × 5 = 0.75
5 − 0.75 = £4.25
Badminton racket:
15 ÷ 100 × 2 = 0.3
2 − 0.3 = £1.70
Shoes:
15 ÷ 100 × 1.2 = 0.18
1.2 − 0.18 = £1.02
Mug:
15 ÷ 100 × 0.8 = 0.12
0.8 − 0.12 = £0.68
b) Set of computer games: £3.00
Video player: £4.30
Badminton racket: £1.70
Shoes: £1.00
Mug: £0.70

Page 57
Q5 a) Total spent on materials: 15.75 + 9.70 + 12.10 = £37.55. She has made 12 pieces of jewellery. 37.55 ÷ 12 = 3.129... so she needs to sell each piece for £3.13 to make her money back.
b) 20% of the cost of materials for one piece is 20 ÷ 100 × 3.13 = 0.63. So she would need to sell each piece for 3.13 + 0.63 = £3.76 to make a 20% profit.
c) If Jess sells all 12 pieces for £3.76 she will have taken 12 × 3.76 = £45.12. She spent £37.55 on materials so will have made 45.12 − 37.55 = £7.57.
Split between 9 hours work, Jess will have made 7.57 ÷ 9 = £0.84 per hour.

Q6 a) It's better for Jess to sell the sculpture online as she is likely to get more money for it (approx. £14.50) than if she sold it at a car boot sale (approx. £10.50).
b) Jess can expect to sell it for approx. £16.50 online and £21.50 at the car boot sale. So she will make 21.50 − 16.50 = £5 more at a car boot sale.
c) Find $y = mx + c$ for the car boot sale graph:
c is the y-intercept, c = 0.
m is the gradient of the line, which is change in y ÷ change in x.
E.g. (25 − 0) ÷ (70 − 0) = 0.36.
So $y = 0.36x$ OR
Price = £0.36 × height in cm.

Page 58
Q7 a) For each litre of petrol, Billy's car travels 8 miles, which costs £1.20. So for each mile Billy travels his car will use 1/8 of a litre, costing 1.20 ÷ 8 = £0.15 (15p). The total cost of petrol and entry can be calculated using the formula C = E + 15d, where C is the total cost in pence, E is the entry fee in pence and d is the distance travelled in miles.
b) Billy needs to pay for entry to sale, plus the cost of travelling to the sale, and home again, so:
Twinton:
C = 500 + (15 × 30) = 950p (£9.50).
Crayforth:
C = 750 + (15 × 24) = 1110p (£11.10).
Wendale:
C = 300 + (15 × 40) = 900p (£9.00).

Answers (Foundation Level): P.59 — P.62

Q8 Total amount in the cash box is £109.78. £30 is left as a float, leaving 109.78 − 30 = £79.78. Billy takes £5.50 to refund himself for the entry cost, leaving 79.78 − 5.50 = £74.28. He also has to refund himself for petrol costs. Total distance travelled will be 34 miles (to the sale and back home again), which will use 34 ÷ 8 = 4.25 litres of petrol (as 8 miles uses 1 litre of petrol). This will cost 4.25 × 1.20 = £5.10 (as 1 litre costs £1.20).
So when Billy takes out petrol money he will be left with 74.28 − 5.10 = £69.18 to split between himself and Gwen.
Billy will receive:
2/3 × 69.18 = £46.12.
Gwen will receive:
1/3 × 69.18 = £23.06.

Banking
Page 59
Q1 a) PGS Bank would pay 10% of £100 = £10.
b) Lomond Bank would pay $\frac{1}{4}$ of £100 = £25.
c) Dylan would save £27 × $\frac{1}{3}$ = £9 on the railcard with PGS Bank.
d) He would get £25 with Lomond Bank and £10 + £9 = £19 with PGS, so his best deal is with Lomond Bank.

Q2 a) Dylan met the target in January, February and May.
b) As he met the target in 3 of the months, he should get:
(£10 × 3) + £15 = £45.

Page 60
Q3 a) The bank will lend Sean:
2.5 × £18 000 = £45 000.
b) 20% of £55 000 =
20 ÷ 100 × £55 000 = £11 000.
So he needs £11 000 − £10 000 = £1000 more.

Q4 a) £1500 ÷ £130 = 11.54 months so it will take him 12 months to save £1500.
b) By May, Sean should have 3 × £130 = £390 already in the account, leaving £1500 − £390 = £1110 left to save. He will have 6 monthly payments before the end of November, so each one should be £1110 ÷ 6 = £185.

Page 61
Q5 a) At the end of one year there will be £2500 + (4% of £2500) in the account.
4% of £2500 = 4 ÷ 100 × £2500 = £100, so total = £2500 + £100 = £2600.
b) After the first year there will be £2600 in the account.
At the end of the second year there will be
£2600 + (4% of £2600)
= £2600 + (4 ÷ 100 × £2600)
= £2600 + £104 = £2704.

Q6 a) Annual interest rate on a 12 month loan of £6750 is 14.5%.
14.5% of £6750 =
14.5 ÷ 100 × £6750 = £978.75.
Total to pay back =
£6750 + £978.75 = £7728.75
b) Each month, Emily will have to pay £7728.75 ÷ 12 months = £644.06 to the nearest penny.

Page 62
Q7 Initial amount = £5000 ÷ (1.05^5)
= £3917.63
= £3918 to the nearest pound.

Q8 E.g. 10 years is not enough so try 11 years:
£3000 × 1.04^{11} = £4618.36.
Too small so try 12 years:
£3000 × 1.04^{12} = £4803.10.
Too small so try 13 years:
£3000 × 1.04^{13} = £4995.22.
Too small so try 14 years:
£3000 × 1.04^{14} = £5195.03.
So it will take Matthew 14 years before he has £5000 in the account.

Guide to Themes and Topics
Higher Level

Getting Around 1
    Q1: *Maps and Scale Drawings, Bearings, Compound Measures (Speed)*
    Q2: *Compound Measures (Speed)*
    Q3: *Compound Measures (Speed)*
    Q4: *Conversion Factors (Metric-Imperial), Compound Measures (Speed)*
    Q5: *Conversion Factors (Metric-Imperial and Currency), Compound Measures (Speed), Two-way Tables*
    Q6: *Conversion Factors (Metric-Imperial)*
    Q7: *Velocity-Time Graphs*
    Q8: *Conversion Factors (Metric-Imperial), Financial Arithmetic*

Food and Drink 5
    Q1: *Conversion Factors (Metric), Fractions, Two-way Tables*
    Q2: *Proportion, Prime Numbers*
    Q3: *Proportion, Conversion Factors (Metric-Imperial)*
    Q4: *Formulas*
    Q5: *Formulas*
    Q6: *Formulas*
    Q7: *Proportion, Fractions*
    Q8: *Ratios, Proportion*

Shopping 9
    Q1: *Financial Arithmetic*
    Q2: *Financial Arithmetic, Proportion*
    Q3: *Two-way Tables, Financial Arithmetic*
    Q4: *Best Buys, Financial Arithmetic*
    Q5: *Best Buys, Financial Arithmetic*
    Q6: *Percentages*
    Q7: *Financial Arithmetic, Fractions*
    Q8: *Fraction Arithmetic, Fractions*

Running a Car 13
    Q1: *Percentages*
    Q2: *Percentages, Financial Arithmetic*
    Q3: *Percentages, Compound Decay*
    Q4: *Conversion Factors (Metric-Imperial), Financial Arithmetic, Percentages*
    Q5: *Compound Decay, Financial Arithmetic*
    Q6: *Histograms, Calculating Averages*
    Q7: *Formulas*
    Q8: *Proportion, Inequalities*

Guide to Themes and Topics
Higher Level

Going Out 17
    Q1: *Percentages, Best Buys, Ratios*
    Q2: *Financial Arithmetic, Fractions*
    Q3: *Financial Arithmetic (Non-Calculator), Fractions, Percentages*
    Q4: *Financial Arithmetic (Non-Calculator), Proportion, Ratios*
    Q5: *Financial Arithmetic (Non-Calculator), Percentages*
    Q6: *Simultaneous Equations*
    Q7: *Financial Arithmetic, Percentages*
    Q8: *Financial Arithmetic, Percentages, Fractions*

Earning and Saving 21
    Q1: *Financial Arithmetic, Percentages*
    Q2: *Percentages, Compound Growth*
    Q3: *Percentages*
    Q4: *Percentages, Compound Growth*
    Q5: *Calculating Averages and Spread, Percentages*
    Q6: *Percentages*
    Q7: *Percentages*
    Q8: *Compound Growth, Percentages*

Holidays 25
    Q1: *Financial Arithmetic, Percentages*
    Q2: *Timings and Timetables*
    Q3: *Formulas, Two-way Tables*
    Q4: *Inequalities, Scales and Measurements, Conversion Factors (Metric-Imperial)*
    Q5: *Volume of 3D Shapes, Conversion Factors (Metric)*
    Q6: *Financial Arithmetic, Timings and Timetables*
    Q7: *Conversion Factors (Metric-Imperial and Currency)*
    Q8: *Maps and Scale Drawings, Conversion Factors (Metric-Imperial), Proportion*

Paying Bills 29
    Q1: *Percentages*
    Q2: *Percentages, Financial Arithmetic*
    Q3: *Proportion, Financial Arithmetic*
    Q4: *Formulas, Conversion Factors (Metric)*
    Q5: *Two-way Tables, Percentages*
    Q6: *Straight Line Graphs*
    Q7: *Proportion*
    Q8: *Compound Growth, Percentages*

Guide to Themes and Topics
Higher Level

Decorating 33
    Q1: *Area, Ratios*
    Q2: *Conversion Factors (Metric-Imperial), Fractions, Financial Arithmetic, Area*
    Q3: *Perimeter, Area, Financial Arithmetic*
    Q4: *Area, Financial Arithmetic*
    Q5: *Calculation Bounds*
    Q6: *Estimating*
    Q7: *Area (including Circles)*
    Q8: *Ratios, Financial Arithmetic*

Safety and Design 37
    Q1: *Nets, Volume of 3D Shapes*
    Q2: *Calculation Bounds*
    Q3: *Pythagoras' Theorem, Financial Arithmetic*
    Q4: *Trigonometry, Area*
    Q5: *Rounding and Accuracy*
    Q6: *Trigonometry, Rounding and Accuracy*
    Q7: *Area, Pythagoras' Theorem, Trigonometry*
    Q8: *Nets, Scale Drawings*

Environmental Issues 41
    Q1: *Calculating Averages and Spread*
    Q2: *Fractions, Financial Arithmetic, Calculating Averages*
    Q3: *Sampling and Data Collection*
    Q4: *Tally Charts, Pie Charts*
    Q5: *Grouped Frequency Tables, Calculating Averages, Percentages*
    Q6: *Conversion Factors (Metric-Imperial), Straight Line Graphs, Financial Arithmetic*

Health and Fitness 44
    Q1: *Calculating Averages and Spread*
    Q2: *Sampling and Data Collection*
    Q3: *Calculating Averages*
    Q4: *Distance-Time Graphs*
    Q5: *Scatter Graphs, Formulas*
    Q6: *Scatter Graphs and Correlation*
    Q7: *Grouped Frequency Tables, Calculating Averages*
    Q8: *Grouped Frequency Tables, Calculating Averages and Spread, Cumulative Frequency Graphs*

Guide to Themes and Topics
Higher Level

Running a Business **49**
- Q1: *Bar Charts, Percentages*
- Q2: *Frequency Polygons, Grouped Frequency Tables, Calculating Averages and Spread*
- Q3: *Straight Line Graphs*
- Q4: *Relative Frequency*
- Q5: *Bar Charts, Percentages, Relative Frequency*
- Q6: *Line Graphs*
- Q7: *Probability, Fractions, Percentages, Line Graphs*
- Q8: *Financial Arithmetic, Percentages*

Hospitals and Healthcare **52**
- Q1: *Probability, Percentages*
- Q2: *Probability, Relative Frequency*
- Q3: *Percentages, Frequency Tables, Calculating Averages, Relative Frequency*
- Q4: *Probability*
- Q5: *Cumulative Frequency Graphs*
- Q6: *Grouped Frequency Tables, Calculating Averages and Spread (Quartliles and Interquartile Range)*

Local Council Issues **55**
- Q1: *Grouped Frequency Tables, Calculating Averages, Percentages*
- Q2: *Sampling and Data Collection*
- Q3: *Calculating Averages*
- Q4: *Pie Charts*
- Q5: *Scale Drawings, Loci and Construction*
- Q6: *Sampling and Data Collection (Stratified Sampling)*
- Q7: *Pie Charts, Percentages*
- Q8: *Cumulative Frequency Graphs, Grouped Frequency Tables, Calculating Averages and Spread*

Science in the Workplace **59**
- Q1: *Standard Index Form*
- Q2: *Standard Index Form, Index Laws*
- Q3: *Volume of 3D Shapes, Conversion Factors (Metric), Rounding and Accuracy, Percentages*
- Q4: *Direct Proportion, Straight Line Graphs*
- Q5: *Inverse Proportion*
- Q6: *Inverse Proportion*
- Q7: *Quadratic Graphs, Formulas*
- Q8: *Quadratic Graphs, Compound Measures (Speed), Conversion Factors (Metric-Imperial)*

Answers (Higher Level): P.1 — P.5

Getting Around
Page 1
Q1 a) 1 cm = 15 000 cm.
15 000 cm ÷ 100 = 150 m,
so 1 cm = 150 m.
b) 253° (allow 250°-255°)
c) 11.2 cm + 8.3 cm + 2.9 cm + 7.6 cm = 30 cm. 1 cm = 150 m, so 30 cm × 150 = 4500 m (allow 4440 m-4560 m).
d) Time = Distance ÷ Speed.
Distance = 4500 m = 4.5 km.
Time = 4.5 km ÷ 10 km/h = 0.45 h. 0.45 h × 60 = 27 mins to the nearest minute.

Q2 a) Time = Distance ÷ Speed.
Hawley to Sampson = 12 ÷ 30 = 0.4 hours × 60 = 24 min.
Sampson to Clay = 8 ÷ 40 = 0.2 hours × 60 = 12 min.
First train leaves at 9.30, takes 24 min, so arrives at Sampson at 9.54 am. 5 min stop so the train leaves Sampson at 9.59 am.
Train takes 12 min from Sampson so arrives at Clay at 10.11 am.
5 min stop so the train leaves Clay at 10.16 am.
b) The 10.00 am train will leave Clay at 10.16 am + 30 min = 10.46 am.
Clay to Turnbull = 6 ÷ 36 = 0.167 hours × 60 = 10 min.
So it will arrive at 10.56 am.

Page 2
Q3 a) Time = Distance ÷ Speed.
= 22 miles ÷ 60 mph
= 0.3666... hours × 60 mins
= 22 mins. It is 19.05, so he will arrive at the ground at 19.27.
b) The shortest time he will take to cover the last 4 miles at 30 mph = 4 ÷ 30 = 0.133... hours × 60 = 8 mins. So he needs to have driven the next (22 miles − 4 miles) = 18 miles, by 19.45 − (8 mins + 15 mins) = 19.22.
This leaves him 17 mins to cover 18 miles.
Speed = 18 miles ÷ (17 mins ÷ 60) = 63.5294... = 64 mph to nearest mph.

Q4 a) 2500 m = 2.5 km. 2.5 km ≈ 2.5 ÷ 1.6 = 1.5625 miles.
102 s ÷ 60 = 1.7 mins ÷ 60 = 0.02833... hours.
Speed = Distance ÷ time
= 1.5625 miles ÷ 0.02833... h
= 55 mph to the nearest mph.
b) Min time = Distance ÷ Max Speed = 1.5625 miles ÷ 50 mph = 0.03125 hours × 60 × 60 = 113 s to the nearest second to pass between the cameras.

Page 3
Q5 a) Total distance travelled:
Plymouth to Exeter to Bristol to Penzance to Plymouth = 44 + 84 + 194 + 77 = 399 miles.
Convert to km:
399 × 1.6 = 638.4 km.
638.4 × 0.65 = €414.96 travel expenses.
b) Last meeting is in Penzance, finishing at 17.30, and Francois needs to travel 77 miles to Plymouth for the ferry.
Time = Distance ÷ Speed
= 77 miles ÷ 60 mph
= 1.2833... h × 60 mins =
77 mins = 1 hour 17 min.
He should arrive in Plymouth at 17.30 + 1 hour 17 min = 18.47, so he should book the next ferry which is at 19.30.

Q6 E.g. Change units of efficiency for both cars to km/litre.
The Gastra travels 51.4 miles per gallon, so approximately 51.4 × 1.6 = 82.24 km per gallon. This is approximately 82.24 ÷ 4.5 = 18.2755... km/litre.
The Vector uses 6.2 litres per 100 km = 100 km ÷ 6.2 litres = 16.1290... km/litre.
Francois should hire the most efficient car, (the car that travels the furthest per litre of fuel) which is the Gastra.

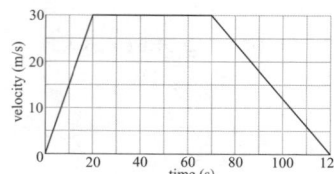

Page 4
Q7

Q8 Total distance = 65 × 2 = 130 miles. 32 miles per gallon, so they will use 130 ÷ 32 = 4.0625 gallons. Convert gallons to litres = 4.0625 × 4.5 = 18.28.. litres.
Diesel costs 120.9p per litre, so 18.28.. × 120.9 = 2210.203..p ÷ 100 = £22.10 for fuel.
Tickets for 25 students: 20 students at £10 each plus two free tickets, plus three students at £10 each = (20 × 10) + (3 × 10) = £230.
Total cost of trip = £22.10 + £230 = £252.10. So the minimum each student should pay is £252.10 ÷ 25 students = £10.10 to the nearest 10p.

Food and Drink
Page 5
Q1 a) There are 12 bread rolls in a pack. June needs 29 white rolls and 21 brown. 29 ÷ 12 = 2.4... so she needs 3 packs of white rolls. 21 ÷ 12 = 1.75, so she needs 2 packs of brown rolls.
b) She needs 13 × 250 ml = 3250 ml cola, and 37 × 250 ml = 9250 ml lemonade. Each bottle holds 2 litres = 2000 ml.
3250 ÷ 2000 = 1.625, so she needs 2 bottles of cola.
9250 ÷ 2000 = 4.625, so she needs 5 bottles of lemonade.
c) She has 5 packets × 5 slices = 25 slices of cheese, which makes 25 cheese rolls. There are 32 + 18 = 50 people in total. One third of these = 50 ÷ 3 = 16.666..., or around 17 people, are vegetarians, so there is enough cheese for the vegetarians.

Q2 a) June's trays are half the depth of the tray recommended in the recipe, but she has 3 of them, so she needs to scale the recipe up by 3 × ½ = 1.5.
Oats: 250 g × 1.5 = 375 g.
Butter: 150 g × 1.5 = 225 g.
Sugar: 75 g × 1.5 = 112.5 g.
Syrup: 75 g × 1.5 = 112.5 g.

Answers (Higher Level): P.6 — P.9

b) 50 slices ÷ 3 trays = 16.666..., so there should be at least 17 slices per tray. 17 is a prime number, so she could only divide the tray up into 17 strips, but these would have a width of 20 cm ÷ 17 = 1.2 cm, which is too thin. The next whole number of slices is 18, which she could divide up as 1 × 18, 2 × 9, or 3 × 6. The only way which has a width of at least 3 cm is to divide the trays into 3 slices by 6 slices, making a total of 18 × 3 = 54 slices of flapjack.

Page 6

Q3 a) Dawn has 8 oz flour on the scales, so she needs to scale the recipe by
8 oz ÷ 12 oz = $\frac{2}{3}$.
Butter: $\frac{2}{3}$ × 9 oz = 6 oz.
Sugar: $\frac{2}{3}$ × 9 oz = 6 oz.
Eggs: $\frac{2}{3}$ × 3 eggs = 2 eggs.
Coffee: $\frac{2}{3}$ × $\frac{3}{4}$ pint = $\frac{1}{2}$ pint.

b) $1\frac{3}{4}$ pints ≈ 1 litre = 1000 ml.
1 pint ≈ 1000 ml ÷ $1\frac{3}{4}$ =
1000 ÷ $\frac{7}{4}$ = 1000 × $\frac{4}{7}$ = $\frac{4000}{7}$ ml.
$\frac{1}{2}$ pint ≈ $\frac{4000}{7}$ × $\frac{1}{2}$ = $\frac{4000}{14}$ ml
= 286 ml to the nearest ml, or 290 ml to the nearest 10 ml.

Q4 a) Dawn needs to reduce the cooking time by 10 mins for every hour.
45 mins = 45 ÷ 60 = 0.75 hours, so she needs to reduce the time by 0.75 × 10 mins = 7.5 mins.
45 mins − 7.5 mins = 38 mins (to the nearest min) to bake the cake.

b) Temp in °F =
($\frac{9}{5}$ × (180 − 25)) + 32 =
($\frac{9}{5}$ × 155) + 32 = 311 °F.

Page 7

Q5 a) Turkey will take
4.5 kg × 2 h per kg = 9 hours to defrost. If Jackson starts to defrost it at 09.15 it will be ready to cook by 18.15. It will take (45 mins × 4.5 kg) + 20 mins = 222.5 mins to cook ≈ 3 h 43 mins, which means it would be ready at 21.58 (9.58 pm), which is too late. So no, there is not enough time to defrost and cook the turkey for 8 pm.

b) Jackson should get home at 6 pm, which means he has 2 hours, or 120 mins, to cook the beef. If the max. weight of beef is b kg, then: 120 mins = (30 mins × b) + 20 mins.
b = (120 − 20) ÷ 30 = 3.33... kg.
So the biggest joint of beef he could buy is 3 kg to the nearest kg.

Q6 a) °F = $\frac{9}{5}$ °C + 32, so rearranging:
°C = $\frac{5}{9}$ × (°F − 32).
°C = $\frac{5}{9}$ × (300 °F − 32) =
148.888 = 149 °C
to the nearest °C.

b) $\frac{5}{9}$ ≈ $\frac{1}{2}$, and 32 ≈ 30, so an approximate formula could be:
°C = $\frac{1}{2}$ × (°F − 30), or in words, subtract 30 then halve.

Page 8

Q7 a) A quarter of the quiche weighs 450 g ÷ 4 = 112.5 g. This contains (271 kcal ÷ 100 g) × 112.5 g = 305 kcal to the nearest kcal.
With a cob of corn:
305 kcal + 105 kcal = 410 kcal, leaving 500 kcal − 410 kcal = 90 kcal for coleslaw.
This means they can each have:
(90 kcal ÷ 140 kcal) × 100 g = 64 g coleslaw, to the nearest g.

b) Without coleslaw, Debbie can have 500 kcal − 105 kcal = 395 kcal in quiche. In the whole quiche there are (271 kcal ÷ 100 g) × 450 g = 1219.5 kcal. This means she can have 395 kcal ÷ 1219.5 kcal = 0.3239... of the quiche, which is approximately one third.

Q8 For the chilli: She needs to scale the recipe up by 30 ÷ 8 = 3.75.
So she needs:
Beef mince: 1 kg × 3.75 = 3.75 kg.
Chopped tomatoes: 800 g × 3.75 = 3000 g = 3 kg.
Red kidney beans: 3 kg.
Onions: 2 × 3.75 = 7.5 = 8 onions.
Garlic cloves: 8 cloves.
Chilli flakes: 4 tsp × 3.75 = 15 tsp.
Cumin: 1 tsp × 3.75 = 3.75 = 4 tsp.
Coriander: 4 tsp.
Rice: 90 g × 30 people = 2700 g or 2.7 kg rice.
Tortilla chips: 30 ÷ 8 = 3.75, so she needs 4 bags.
For the cocktails:
She needs 300 ml × 30 = 9000 ml in total, split in ratio 5 : 2 : 1. Total number of parts = 5 + 2 + 1 = 8 parts. Each part is 9000 ml ÷ 8 = 1125 ml.
Lemonade: 5 × 1125 ml = 5625 ml.
Lime juice: 2 × 1125 ml = 2250 ml.
Orange syrup: 1125 ml.

Shopping
Page 9

Q1 a) 5 l + 1 l = £5.99 + £1.99 = £7.98.
Three tins of 2 l = 3 × £2.99 = £8.97, so the cheapest way is to buy a 5 litre tin and a 1 litre tin.

b) John could buy three 5 m rolls for 3 × £9 = £27, an 8 m roll and a 5 m roll for £18 + £9 = £27, or a 10 m roll for £25, so the 10 m roll is the cheapest.

c) (60 × £0.95) + (40 × £0.80) + (15 × £1.95) + (10 × £1.45) = £132.75.

Answers (Higher Level): P.10 — P.13

Q2 a) Apples: £1.69 per kg.
648 g ÷ 1000 = 0.648 kg.
£1.69 × 0.648 kg = 1.095...
= £1.10, so she has been overcharged for the apples.
Soft drinks: 0.59 + 0.59 − 0.08 = £1.10, so she has been charged the right amount for the soft drinks.
Crisps:
0.79 + 0.79 + 0.79 − 0.16 = £2.21, so she has been overcharged for the crisps.

b) Apples should be £1.10.
Drinks should be £1.10.
Crisps should be £2. So she should have been charged £1.10 + £1.10 + £2 = £4.20.

c) £10 − £4.20 = £5.80 change.
£5.80 ÷ 4 = £1.45 each for Joe and each of his sisters.

Page 10

Q3 a) Digitalmemcards.co.uk: £19.99.
Bestvaluememory.co.uk:
£12.99 + £1.50 = £14.49.
Memcd.co.uk: £15.99.
allcostsless.co.uk:
£14.98 + £1.25 = £16.23.
So he should buy it from Bestvaluememory.co.uk.

b) He bought the 1 GB card for £8.12. The cheapest elsewhere is £6.58. Difference = £8.12 − £6.58 = £1.54, double the difference = £1.54 × 2 = £3.08, so they should refund him £3.08.

Q4 a) 55 + 95 = 150 photos.
PrintBest:
(150 × 6p) + £2 = £11.
PrintCheaper:
(150 × 7p) + £1.50 = £12.
CheapoPrint: 150 × 8p = £12.
So they should use PrintBest to get the cheapest deal.

b) 95 photos at 6p each = 95 × £0.06 = £5.70, plus half P&P cost = £2 ÷ 2 = £1. So she owes him £5.70 + £1 = £6.70.

Page 11

Q5 a) To find best value, work out price per ml or per g.
Drinks:
Big Fizz: 149p ÷ 2000 ml = 0.0745p/ml.
Hot Fizz Deal: 200p ÷ 3000 ml = 0.0667p/ml.
Can: 80p ÷ 330 ml = 0.2424p/ml.
6 Pack Cans: 180p ÷ (6 × 330 ml) = 0.0909p/ml
So the best value drink is the '2 for £2' deal on Hot Fizz.
Snacks:
Mega Bag: 199p ÷ 300 g = 0.6633p/g.
Snack in the Box Deal:
(2 × 165p) ÷ (3 × 230 g) = 0.4783p/g.
Pic n Mix: 99p ÷ 100 g = 0.99p/g.
So the best value for snacks is the '3 for 2' Snack in the Box deal.

b) The minimum Lina has to spend for the best value options is £2 (for the Hot Fizz deal) + (2 × £1.65) (for the Snacks deal) = £5.30, so no, it is not possible to buy them for £5.

Q6 a) 5% of £12 = (5 ÷ 100) × £12 = £0.60. So each sale DVD costs £12 − £0.60 = £11.40.
Buying three will cost:
(£11.40 × 3) − 5% = £34.20 − (5 ÷ 100 × £34.20) = £32.49.
Buying five will cost:
(£11.40 × 5) − 10% = £57 − (10 ÷ 100 × £57) = £51.30, which is more than £50.
Buying four will cost:
£32.49 + £11.40 = £43.89, so the most Lina could buy for £50 is 4 DVDs.

b) Five sale DVDs cost £51.30.
Five non-sale DVDs cost
(£12 × 5) − 12% = £60 − (12 ÷ 100 × £60) = £52.80. So it is cheaper for Lina to choose from the sale DVDs.

Page 12

Q7 Total cost of stationery:
£0.95 + £1.50 + (£2.25 × 2) + £2 + £2.99 + (£1.99 × 2) + (£1.99 × 2) + (£1.20 × 6) + £4.99 + £0.50 = £32.59. With the £10 off voucher:
£32.59 − £10 = £22.59.
With the $\frac{1}{3}$ off deal:
£32.59 × $\frac{1}{3}$ = £10.86.
£32.59 − £10.86 = £21.73.
The least amount James could spend is £21.73 if he uses the $\frac{1}{3}$ off offer.

Q8 August = 31 days.
Dog food: ⅔ tin × 2 dogs = 1⅓ tins × 31 days = 41⅓ tins in total, so she will have to buy 42 tins. She should buy 3 packs of 12 tins = 3 × £7.99 = £23.97, plus 6 tins at 80p each = 6 × £0.80 = £4.80.
£23.97 + £4.80 = £28.77.
Cat food: ¼ tin × 3 cats = ¾ tin twice a day = 1.5 tins × 31 days = 46.5 tins, so she will have to buy 47 tins.
She should buy 1 box of 36 tins for £20, 1 pack of 10 tins for £6 and 1 tin for 70p. £20 + £6 + £0.70 = £26.70.
Fish food: she should buy 2 packets, 2 × £1.19 = £2.38.
Total = £28.77 + £26.70 + £2.38 = £57.85, so yes she can buy it all.

Running a Car
Page 13

Q1 a) 17.5% of £135 = 0.175 × £135 = £23.63, so total cost = £135 + £23.63 = £158.63.

b) MOT + Full Service = £55 + £158.63 = £213.63.
10% of £213.63 = 0.1 × £213.63 = £21.36. So with the discount it would cost £213.63 − £21.36 = £192.27.

c) Total cost for service, MOT and tax = £192.27 + £125 = £317.27.

Answers (Higher Level):   P.14 — P.17

Q2 a) With Insure-Ants, Mark would pay £467 − (20% of £467) = £467 − (0.2 × £467) = £373.60. With Chassis-Sure, Mark would pay £434 − (10% of £434) = £434 − (0.1 × £434) = £390.60. So the cheapest quote for Mark is £373.60 with Insure-Ants.
b) £373.60 + (7.5% of £373.60) = £373.60 + (0.075 × £373.60) = £401.62. Lowest monthly payment = £401.62 ÷ 12 = £33.47.

Page 14
Q3 a) Deposit is 20% of £11 499 = 0.2 × £11 499 = £2299.80. Each month Sarah would have to pay: (£11 499 − £2299.80) ÷ 24 = £383.30.
b) Final payment with Option 2 would be £11 499 − (36 × £199) = £4335.
c) 36 months ÷ 12 = 3 years. Using compound decay, after 3 years the value will be: £11 499 × (1 − 0.15)^3 = £11 499 × 0.85^3 = £7061.82.

Q4 a) Milo and Danni each do 10 return trips to work = 40 journeys in total per month. Each journey is 10 miles. 1 mile = 1.6 km, so 10 miles = 16 km. 40 × 16 km = 640 km per month in total.
b) Amount of fuel used in total = (640 km ÷ 100) × 6 litres per 100 km = 38.4 litres. Cost of fuel = 38.4 litres × 119.9p = 4604.16p = £46.04 per month.
c) Each person should be paying £46.04 ÷ 3 = £15.35 per month. Darren wants to pay 10% more and split it between the drivers. £15.35 + (0.1 × £15.35) = £16.89. £16.89 ÷ 2 = £8.45, so Darren should pay the others £8.50 each per month.

Page 15
Q5 Cost of Repairs:
Exhaust = £290,
Brakes = 2 × (£39 + £59) = £196,
Tyres = £95, Suspension = £98,
Tracking = £62,
Total = £741.
Value of the car = £10 500 × (1 − 0.22)^9 = £1122.12. £1122.12 × $\frac{2}{3}$ = £748.08. This is more than the cost of the repairs, so Alun should not scrap his car.

Q6 From the histogram, the frequency of each group is the area of the bar, so:

Price p (£)	Freq.
0 ≤ p < 1000	1 × 1000 = 1000
1000 ≤ p < 1250	10 × 250 = 2500
1250 ≤ p < 1500	7 × 250 = 1750
1500 ≤ p < 1750	6 × 250 = 1500
1750 ≤ p < 2000	5 × 250 = 1250
2000 ≤ p < 3000	1.5 × 1000 = 1500
3000 ≤ p < 3500	1 × 500 = 500

The median price would be at (10 000 + 1) ÷ 2 = 5000.5th place, i.e. somewhere within the £1250-£1500 price range, which means £1750 can not be the median value, so the seller's argument is not correct.

Page 16
Q7 For the 19 mile journey Paul should claim:
£3.20 + (19 × £0.16) = £6.24.
For the 42 mile journey he should claim: £8 + ((42 − 30) × £0.10) = £9.20. So in total he should claim £6.24 + £9.20 = £15.44.

Q8 A full tank costs 55 litres × 119.9p = £65.95. This will last for 425 miles, so Paul actually pays £65.95 ÷ 425 = £0.16 per mile for petrol. For long journeys, distance m miles, the company pay £8 + £0.1(m − 30), and he pays £0.16m, so Paul is only being paid enough if:
8 + 0.1(m − 30) ≥ 0.16m.
Solving this for m gives:
8 + 0.1m − 3 ≥ 0.16m
5 ≥ 0.06m
5 ÷ 0.06 ≥ m
83.3 ≥ m, or m ≤ 83 to the nearest mile.
This means that Paul is only being paid enough for journeys of up to 83 miles. If he travels more than 83 miles, the money he can claim will not cover his petrol costs.

Going Out
Page 17
Q1 a) Costs per ml:
Glass — 179 ÷ 275 = 0.65p
Jug — 350 ÷ 650 = 0.54p
Pitcher — 555 ÷ 1000 = 0.56p
so the jug is the best deal.
b) Costs per ml:
Glass — 149p ÷ 275 ml = 0.54p
Jug — first find the price during happy hour, then the cost per ml. 10% of 305p = 10 ÷ 100 × 305p = 30.5p, so discount price = 305p − 30.5p = 274.5p.
274.5p ÷ 650 ml = 0.42p
Pitcher — 460p ÷ 1000 ml = 0.46p.
So the jug is the best value.
c) Natalie, Claire and Nicky drank in the ratio 2 : 2 : 1, so the total needs to be split into 2 + 2 + 1 = 5 parts. £18.70 ÷ 5 = £3.74. So Natalie and Claire each owe £3.74 × 2 = £7.48, and Nicky owes £3.74.

Answers (Higher Level): P.18 — P.21

Q2 a) Using the 2 for 1 offer, 3 tickets would cost:
£23.50 + £23.50 + £0.00 = £47.
Using the buy 1 get 1 half price and a third off an adult would cost: £23.50 + (£23.50 ÷ 2) + £23.50 − ($\frac{1}{3}$ × £23.50) = £50.92
So they should use the 2 for 1 offer to get the cheapest tickets.

b) Each of the girls should pay 47 ÷ 3 = £15.6666....
So Nicky owes 15.6666... ÷ 2 = £7.83 to each of the other girls, to the nearest penny.

Page 18

Q3 a) 1 family ticket and one child's ticket cost £20 + £4.50 = £24.50. With the 15% discount, each adult ticket will cost: £6.50 − (15 ÷ 100 × £6.50) = £5.53 (to the nearest penny). So 2 discounted adult's tickets and 3 child's tickets will cost: (2 × £5.53) + (3 × £4.50) = £24.56. So it is cheaper to buy 1 family ticket and 1 child's ticket.

b) 1 combo plus 1 drink and 2 popcorns will cost:
£4.10 + £2.99 + (2 × £2.89) = £12.87.
2 combos plus 1 popcorn will cost: (2 × £4.10) + £2.89 = £11.09.
3 combos will cost 3 × £4.10 = £12.30.
So the cheapest way is to buy 2 combos and 1 additional popcorn.

c) Discounted ticket price = £4.50 − ($\frac{1}{3}$ × £4.50) = £3, so the tickets will cost £3 + £4.50 = £7.50.
Individual drinks and popcorn will cost (2 × £2.99) + (2 × £2.89) = £11.76.
A combo and an extra popcorn will cost £4.10 + £2.89 = £6.99.
So the minimum amount of money needed is £7.50 + £6.99 = £14.49.

Q4 a) There are 12 people in total, so price per person: £84.70 ÷ 12 = £7.058....
Cohens owe £7.058... × 5 = 35.29.
Robinsons owe £7.058... × 4 = £28.23.
Lewseys owe £7.058... × 3 = 21.18.

b) 6 are sharing the cost of the drinks bill so price per person: £47.10 ÷ 6 = £7.85.
Cohens owe £7.85 × 3 = £23.55.
Robinsons owe £7.85.
Lewseys owe £7.85 × 2 = £15.70.

Page 19

Q5 a) Josh owes money for 1 spag. bol. and 2 orange juices, as well as $\frac{1}{3}$ of the cost of two garlic breads.
So he owes £7.80 + (2 × £1.10) + ($\frac{1}{3}$ × (2 × £4.25)) = £12.833...
10% tip = 10 ÷ 100 × £12.833... = £1.2833...
He should leave £12.833... + £1.2833... = £14.12.

b) Jason also owes £12.83. If he pays by card he'll be charged: 5 ÷ 100 × £12.83 = £0.64 extra. If he withdraws cash he'll be charged £1.25, so it's cheaper for him to pay by card.

Q6 a) The price of a coffee (c) and the price of a tea (t) can be found by solving simultaneous equations:
(1) $2c + t = 3.90$ and
(2) $c + 2t = 3.75$.
(1) × 2 gives: (3) $4c + 2t = 7.80$
(3) − (2) leaves: $3c = 4.05$
$c = 4.05 ÷ 3 = 1.35$,
so 1 cup of coffee costs £1.35.

b) In equation (2),
$c + 2t = 3.75$
$1.35 + 2t = 3.75$
$2t = 3.75 − 1.35 = 2.40$
$t = 2.40 ÷ 2 = 1.20$, so 1 cup of tea costs £1.20. So:
Samantha owes 2 × £1.20 = £2.40
Sarah owes 2 × £1.35 = £2.70
Miriam owes £1.20 + £1.35 = £2.55.

Page 20

Q7 Toby's budget is £20 × 12 = £240.
Cost of joining Lockwick LARPers:
- 12 months of fees with one month free = £9 × 11 = £99.
- Equipment hire is either (£14.99 × 15 events) = £224.85, or £139 for the year, which is cheaper.
- Total cost = £99 + £139 = £238.

Cost of joining the tennis club:
- Membership costs £120, plus £2.50 each week = £120 + (£2.50 × 52) = £250.
- Cheapest racket is £29 with a 25% discount: £29 − (25 ÷ 100 × £29) = £21.75.
- Total cost = £250 + £21.75 = £271.75.

So Toby can afford to join Lockwick LARPers but not Sparkham Tennis Club.

Q8 Transport costs:
£15.60 − ($\frac{1}{3}$ × £15.60) = £10.40.
Animal park costs:
£15 − (30 ÷ 100 × £15) = £10.50.
Lunch costs £5.
Total cost = £10.40 + £10.50 + £5 = £25.90. So Toby will need to withdraw £30.

Earning and Saving
Page 21

Q1 a) Weekly wages:
Laundry assistant = 12 h × £8.50 = £102.
Dog groomer = 16 h × £8.25 = £132.
Bricklayer = 15 h × £8.40 = £126.
So the dog groomer job will pay the most per week.

b) The most Annika could save is: 60% of (£132 per week × 12 wks) = (60 ÷ 100) × £132 × 12 = £950.40.

c) £6475 ÷ 52 weeks = £124.52 per week. The dog groomer and bricklayer jobs both pay more than this so tax would be deducted from her wages with these jobs.

Answers (Higher Level): P.22 — P.24

Q2 a) £800 + (5% of £800)
= £800 + (0.05 × £800)
= £800 × 1.05 = £840.
b) £800 × 1.05³ = £926.10, so Willem won't have enough to go travelling.

Page 22

Q3 a) If she makes £15 000 of sales she will earn 4% of £15 000 as commission + (£21 000 ÷ 12) basic salary per month:
(0.04 × £15 000) + (£21 000 ÷ 12) = £600 + £1750 = £2350.
b) Gabby's basic salary is £1750 per month, so she needs £3000 − £1750 = £1250 in commission. If this was at the 4% rate, then: 4% of sales = £1250. 100% of sales = £1250 ÷ 4 × 100 = £31 250, but this amount would be at a higher % rate, so try 6%:
6% of sales = £1250
100% of sales = £1250 ÷ 6 × 100 = £20 833 to the nearest pound. This is in the right % rate, so this is the amount she needs to make each month in sales.

Q4 a) Total annual earnings = £30 255. So the bank should lend Gabby 2.5 × £30 255 = £75 638 to the nearest pound.
b) The savings bond has had £12 000 earning 4% interest for 8 years, so it should contain: £12 000 × 1.04⁸ = £16 422.83.
c) Using the money in the bond as a 20% deposit, the most expensive flat she could buy with this deposit is:
£16 423 ÷ 20% × 100% = £82 115. For this she would need to borrow £82 115 − £16 423 = £65 692 from the bank, which is less than the maximum allowed, so she could afford a flat costing £82 115.

Page 23

Q5 a) E.g. Total salaries for the 15 employees = £266 100. Mean salary = £266 100 ÷ 15 = £17 740.
A 5% increase = 5 ÷ 100 × £17 740 = £887.
This is less than £1000, so increasing each salary by £1000 gives the bigger mean salary.
b) Currently the highest salary is £38 000, and the lowest is £10 200. A 5% increase would make the highest salary = £38 000 + (0.05 × £38 000) = £39 900, and the lowest salary = £10 200 + (0.05 × £10 200) = £10 710. This would mean the range of salaries was:
£39 900 − £10 710 = £29 190.
A £1000 increase would make the highest salary £39 000, and the lowest £11 200. This would give a range of:
£39 000 − £11 200 = £27 800.
So the £1000 increase gives the smallest range of salaries.
c) Current total salary = £266 100. Mr Bigge has an extra £280 000 − £266 100 = £13 900 to give a pay rise, so they can all get a maximum of £13 900 ÷ 15 = £927 to the nearest £1.

Q6 a) £200 per month = £200 × 12 = £2400 per year. This is £2400 ÷ £34 000 × 100% = 7.1% of her salary, so the maximum she can afford is Option B. With Option B, 12% of her salary will be added to her pension each year:
12 ÷ 100 × £34 000 = £4080.
b) For the paying out options, the total amounts paid out over 20 years are as follows:
X: £4000 + (0.15 × £34 000 × 20) = £106 000.
Y: £10 000 + (0.1 × £34 000 × 20) = £78 000.
Z: 0.2 × £34 000 × 20 = £136 000.
So Option Z gives the highest total amount.

Page 24

Q7 a) Pierce would have paid 20% annual tax of
(£12 000 − £6475) = 0.2 × (£12 000 − £6475) = £1105. He worked for 9 months so in total he would have paid £1105 ÷ 12 months × 9 months = £828.75.
b) His actual salary was £12 000 ÷ 12 × 9 = £9000 for the whole year. He should have only paid tax of: 0.2 × (£9000 − £6475) = £505. So he can claim back £828.75 − £505 = £323.75 in overpaid taxes.

Q8 For the Fixed Interest Account, amount in the account at the end of each year (Y) can be calculated as follows:
Y1: £10 000 × 1.055 = £10 550
Y2: £10 550 × 1.055 = £11 130.25
Y3: £11 130.25 × 1.055 = £11 742.41
Y4: £11 742.41 × 1.055 = £12 388.25
Y5: £12 388.25 × 1.055 = £13 069.60
So Rich would reach his target in 5 years.
For the Growing Interest Account:
Y1: £10 000 × 1.02 = £10 200
Y2: £10 200 × 1.03 = £10 506
Y3: £10 506 × 1.04 = £10 926.24
Y4: £10 926.24 × 1.05 = £11 472.55
Y5: £11 472.55 × 1.06 = £12 160.91
Y6: £12 160.91 × 1.07 = £13 012.17
It would take 6 years to reach his target with this account, so Rich should choose the Fixed Interest Account.

Answers (Higher Level): P.25 — P.29

Holidays
Page 25
Q1 a) Total cost of holiday:
£633 × 3 = £1899.
Deposit: 20 ÷ 100 × 1899 = £379.80.
  b) Balance: £1899 − £379.80 = £1519.20. Each instalment: £1519.20 ÷ 8 = £189.90.
  c) She saves £200 each month. £189.90 of this will be used to pay the balance. £200 − £189.90 = £10.10 will be left over to go towards car hire. At the end of eight months she will have £10.10 × 8 = £80.80 to hire a car, so she will be able to hire the Rentault Standard or the Folkswagon Basic.

Q2 a) They need to leave the house 90 + 45 = 135 mins before their departure time. 135 mins = 2 hrs 15 mins, so the latest they can leave is 12:20.
  b) The plane departs at 14:35 and travels for 2 hrs 50 mins, so lands at 17:25 UK time. Spain is 1 hour ahead so the earliest they can collect the car is 18:25.

Page 26
Q3 a) (77 − 32) × 5/9 = 25 °C.
  b) Joe is wrong to make this assumption. The information in the guidebook only tells him the average temperature, not the range of temperatures. If the range of temperatures is large then he may need clothes for cooler weather too.

Q4 a) Joe's luggage weighs 23 lbs. 23 lbs is (23 ÷ 2.2) kg = 10.5 kg so there will be no excess charge.
Mr Thompson's luggage weighs 37 lbs. 37 lbs is (37 ÷ 2.2) kg = 16.8 kg so an excess of £42 will be charged. Mrs Thompson's luggage weighs 27 lbs. 27 lbs is (27 ÷ 2.2) kg = 12.3 kg so there will be no excess charge. So they will have to pay £42 in total.
  b) Mr Thompson's bag needs to be 13.5 kg or less so 16.8 − 13.5 = 3.3 kg needs to be taken out. Joe's bag can take an additional 13.5 − 10.5 = 3.0 kg. This leaves 3.3 − 3.0 = 0.3 kg that can be added to Mrs Thompson's bag. So 3.0 × 2.2 = 6.6 lbs can be taken out of Mr Thompson's bag and added to Joe's bag. 0.3 × 2.2 = 0.66 lbs can be taken out of Mr Thompson's bag and added to Mrs Thompson's. (Other methods and answers are possible.)

Page 27
Q5 1 litre = 1000 cm^3 so volume of bag A is 62 400 cm^3, volume of bag B is 41 000 cm^3 and volume of bag C is 28 000 cm^3. Use these volumes to find the missing dimensions.
Bag A:
42 × 55 × depth = 62 400.
Depth = 62 400 ÷ (42 × 55).
Depth = 27.0 cm.
Bag B:
20 × 50 × depth = 41 000.
Depth = 41 000 ÷ (20 × 50).
Depth = 41 cm.
Bag C:
53 × 22 × depth = 28 000.
Depth = 28 000 ÷ (53 × 22).
Depth = 24.0 cm.
So the Thompsons could buy bags B and C to use as hand luggage as they meet the size restrictions.

Q6 a) Cost of organised tour:
10% of €85 = 10 ÷ 100 × €85 = €8.50. So it would cost €85 − €8.50 = €76.50.
Cost of the trip independently:
Entry costs + lunch + bus pass = €20 + €10 + €6 = €36.
So Joe would save €76.50 − €36 = €40.50.
  b) The earliest time Joe would get to the Roman museum is 11:30. If he spends 2.5 hours there he would get the 14:30 bus to the amphitheatre and arrive there at 14:45. Spending 2 hours there would take him to 16:45. The last bus is at 16:30 so Joe wouldn't be able to spend the amount of time at the attractions that he wanted if he travelled independently.

Page 28
Q7 4 oz = 4 ÷ 16 = 0.25 lbs. So the ham she wants to buy is 5.25 lbs.
Price in the UK:
5.25 × 35.20 = £184.80.
Price in Spain:
5.25 lbs = (5.25 ÷ 2.2) kg = 2.39 kg. 2.39 × 75.60 = €180.68.
Convert €s to £s:
180.68 ÷ 1.16 = £155.76.
So she would save 184.80 − 155.76 = £29.04.

Q8 Distance on map is approx 3.6 cm which is 3.6 × 25 = 90 km.
90 km = 90 ÷ 1.6 miles = 56.25 miles.
1 gallon is 1 ÷ 0.22 = 4.55 litres. So the car does 48 miles per 4.55 litres. The family need to travel 56.25 miles so need 4.55/48 × 56.25 litres of petrol, which is 5.33 litres.
This will cost 1.18 × 5.33 = €6.29.

Paying Bills
Page 29
Q1 a) Potteries Power will give a discount of 7.5% on £446.72, so Aimee can expect to pay:
£446.72 − (7.5 ÷ 100 × £446.72) = £413.22.
  b) General Generators will give a discount of 17.5% on £186.21, so Aimee can expect to pay:
£186.21 − (17.5 ÷ 100 × £186.21) = £153.62.
  c) With Potteries Power, Aimee would pay £186.21 + £413.22 = £599.43.
With General Generators she would pay £446.72 + £153.62 = £600.34. So she should choose Potteries Power.

Answers (Higher Level): P.30 — P.32

Q2 a) £973.80 is only 75% of the full cost. So without the discount the full amount (100%) would be: £973.80 ÷ 75% × 100% = £1298.40.

b) Half of the council tax bill is £1298.40 ÷ 2 = £649.20. Each month this would cost £649.20 ÷ 12 = £54.10. So Emma should pay Aimee: £54.10 + £180 + £40 = £274.10 per month.

Page 30

Q3 a) In total, Dave and Kate earn £1750 + £1400 = £3150.
Dave earns: £1750 ÷ £3150 = $\frac{5}{9}$
Kate earns: £1400 ÷ £3150 = $\frac{4}{9}$
so the bills can be split as follows:

Bills	Dave Pays:	Kate Pays:
Rent	£540 × 5 ÷ 9 = £300	£540 − £300 = £240
Gas	£45.00 × 5 ÷ 9 = £25.00	£45.00 − £25.00 = £20.00
Electric	£27.45 × 5 ÷ 9 = £15.25	£27.45 − £15.25 = £12.20
Water	£20.25 × 5 ÷ 9 = £11.25	£20.25 − £11.25 = £9.00
Phone / Net	£18.90 × 5 ÷ 9 = £10.50	£18.90 − £10.50 = £8.40
C-Tax	£99.90 × 5 ÷ 9 = £55.50	£99.90 − £55.50 = £44.40

b) E.g. In total, Dave pays: £300.00 + £25.00 + £15.25 + £11.25 + £10.50 + £55.50 = £417.50 for bills, which leaves him with £1750 − £417.50 = £1332.50.
In total, Kate pays: £240.00 + £20.00 + £12.20 + £9.00 + £8.40 + £44.40 = £334.00 for bills, which leaves her with £1400 − £334.00 = £1066.00.

Q4 Each year, Dave and Kate would use in total: 155 litres × 2 × 365 days = 113 150 litres. 1000 litres is 1 m³ so they would use 113 150 ÷ 1000 = 113.15 m³ per year. With a water meter they would pay:
(12 × £2.70) + (113.15 m³ × £1.25) = £173.84.
Currently they pay £20.25 × 12 = £243 per year, so they would save £243 − £173.84 = £69.16 per year.

Page 31

Q5 a) On the Dungbeetle tariff, Joe would pay:
£10 + (£0.20 × 272 mins) + (£0.12 × (374 − 100) texts) + 17.5% VAT = £97.28 + (0.175 × £97.28) = £114.30.
On the Earwig tariff he would pay: £15 + (£0.15 × (272 − 100 mins) + (£0.10 × (374 − 200) texts) + 17.5% VAT = £58.20 + (0.175 × £58.20) = £68.39.
On the Praying Mantis tariff he would pay: £25 + (£0.05 × (272 − 200) mins) + 17.5% VAT = £28.60 + (0.175 × £28.60) = £33.61.
So Praying Mantis is the cheapest tariff for Joe.

b) On the Praying Mantis tariff, with the 10% discount, Joe would have paid:
£33.61 − (0.1 × £33.61) = £30.25. This is a saving of £85.96 − £30.25 = £55.71 on his last bill.

Q6 a)

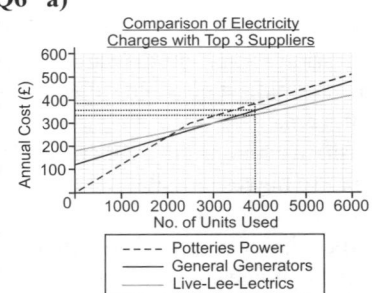

Comparison of Electricity Charges with Top 3 Suppliers
(graph: Annual Cost (£) vs No. of Units Used; lines for Potteries Power, General Generators, Live-Lee-Lectrics)

From the graph, at 3874 units, Live-Lee-Lectrics is the cheapest.

b) The smaller supplier would charge: (£12.50 × 12) + (£0.07 × 3874) = £421.18. This is more expensive than the cheapest of the three other suppliers so it is not cheaper to use this smaller supplier.

Page 32

Q7 Two of the five have big rooms, so the rent is split into 1.5 + 1 + 1 + 1.5 + 1 = 6 parts. Each part is £1350 ÷ 6 = £225.
So the rent is £225 for a small room, and £225 × 1.5 = £337.50 for a big room.
The TV licence is split between 2 people who have TVs, so they will each pay £12.20 ÷ 2 = £6.10 per month.
The internet is split between 3 people who want it, so they will each pay £14.70 ÷ 3 = £4.90.
The amount each person has to pay per month is:
Ben: £337.50 + £6.10 + £4.90 = £348.50.
Trevor: £225.
Tom: £225 + £4.90 = £229.90.
Luke: £337.50.
Fiona: £225 + £6.10 + £4.90 = £236.

Q8 a) With Plan A, interest is charged for the last 9 months of the year, at a rate of 1.5% per month. Balance after 12 months = £1500 × (1 + 0.015)^9 = £1715.08. Interest = £1715.08 − £1500 = £215.08.
With Plan B, interest is charged for the last 6 months of the year, at a rate of 2% per month. Balance after 12 months = £1500 × (1 + 0.02)^6 = £1689.24.
Interest = £1689.24 − £1500 = £189.24.
So Plan B will charge him the least amount of interest in total.

b) If he chooses Plan B, which charges the least interest, he will pay off 60% of £1689.24 after 12 months.
60 ÷ 100 × £1689.24 = £1013.54, which leaves £1689.24 − £1013.54 = £675.70.
Before he pays this off, interest will be charged at 2%:
2 ÷ 100 × £675.70 = £13.51.
So the lowest total amount he will have to pay is £1689.24 + £13.51 = £1702.75.

Answers (Higher Level): P.33 — P.37

Decorating
Page 33
Q1 a) Area of trapezium wall:
½(4.2 + 5.1) × 2.0 = 9.3 m².
Area of rectangular wall:
2.0 × 3.3 = 6.6 m².
Total area:
(2 × 9.3) + 6.6 = 25.2 m².
b) For one coat: 25.2 ÷ 14 = 1.8 litres. For two coats, need: 1.8 × 2 = 3.6 litres.
c) For paint ratio 7 : 2, there are 9 parts, with 7 parts white paint. Total amount of white needed: (3.6 litres ÷ 9 parts) × 7 parts = 2.8 litres. So she needs: 2.8 − 1.2 = 1.6 litres.

Q2 a) Change to cm by ÷ 10:
Height = 150 cm,
Width = 100 cm.
Then ÷ 2.5 to change to inches:
Height = 150 ÷ 2.5 = 60 inches
Width = 100 ÷ 2.5 = 40 inches.
b) Glass height = (60 − (5 × ½)) ÷ 4 = 57½ ÷ 4 = $14\frac{3}{8}$ in.
Glass width = (40 − (5 × ½)) ÷ 4 = 37½ ÷ 4 = $9\frac{3}{8}$ in.
c) Need 16 panes of glass, each with area ($14\frac{3}{8}$ × $9\frac{3}{8}$) = $134\frac{49}{64}$ in².
Approximate cost at 10p per in²: $134\frac{49}{64}$ × 16 × £0.10 = £215.63.
So no, it isn't enough to pay for the panes.

Page 34
Q3 a) On drawing, perimeter of room is 28 cm and door is 0.8 cm wide, so at a scale of 1:100, perimeter of actual room is 28 m and the door is 0.8 m wide. Length of skirting required = 28 − 0.8 = 27.2 m. Will need 28 metre lengths, so cost = 28 × £2.75 = £77.
b) Floor area = (6 × 4.8) + (2.8 × 3.2) = 37.76 m².
Laminate flooring is cheaper by £3 per m², so she will save: 37.76 × £3 = £113.28.

Q4 a) Area to be painted or wallpapered is the total area of the four walls less the area of the two doors:
Area = 4(3.2 × 2.6) − 2(2.1 × 0.8) = 29.92 m².
b) To paper the walls:
Area covered by 1 roll = 9 × 0.8 = 7.2 m².
Minimum no. of rolls needed = 29.92 ÷ 7.2 = 4.2, so 5 rolls.
Minimum cost of paper = 5 × £11.50 = £57.50.
To paint the walls:
No. of tins = (29.92 ÷ 28) × 2 coats = 2.1, so 3 tins.
Cost of paint = 3 × £15 = £45.
So it's more expensive to wallpaper the room.
c) Area to be wallpapered = 3.2 × 2.6 = 8.32 m².
Area to be painted = 29.92 − 8.32 = 21.6 m².
No. rolls paper needed = 8.32 ÷ 7.2 = 1.2, so 2 rolls.
Cost of paper = 2 × £11.50 = £23.
No. tins of paint needed = (21.6 ÷ 28) × 2 coats = 1.5, so 2 tins.
Cost of paint = 2 × £15 = £30.
Total cost = £23 + £30 = £53.

Page 35
Q5 Gap width = 121 cm to nearest cm, so smallest possible value = 120.5 cm.
Wash. machine width = 60 cm to 2 s.f., so biggest possible value is 60.5 cm.
Tumble Drier width = 600 mm to 2 s.f., so biggest possible value is 605 mm = 60.5 cm.
Biggest combined width of appliances = 60.5 + 60.5 = 121 cm, which would not fit into gap of 120.5 cm. So Charlie can not be certain that both appliances will fit in the gap.

Q6 E.g. Tiles are approx. 20 cm by 23 cm, so need around 20 × 10 = 200 to tile the wall. Box contains approx. 25 tiles, so need ≈ 200 ÷ 25 = 8 boxes.
Area of wall ≈ 2.5 m × 4 m = 10 m². Adhesive covers approx. 4 m² per tub so need 10 m² ÷ 4 ≈ 3 tubs.
Cost ≈ (8 boxes × £15 per box) + (3 tubs × £11 per tub) = £120 + £33 = £153.

Page 36
Q7 Area of rectangular paths = (13.0 × 0.5) + (6.5 × 0.5) = 9.75 m².
Area of quarter circle = ¼(π × 4²) = 4π m². Total area = 9.75 + 4π = 22.32 m².
Gravel required = 22.32 m² ÷ 25 m² per tonne = 0.893 tonnes = 893 kg = 890 kg to the nearest 10 kg.

Q8 To make concrete, split 1500 kg in the ratio 6 : 3 : 2 : 1.
Total no. of parts = 12.
Each part = 1500 ÷ 12 = 125 kg.
6 parts Gravel = 6 × 125 = 750 kg.
3 parts Sand = 3 × 125 = 375 kg.
2 parts Cement = 2 × 125 = 250 kg.
(Don't need to work out water as it doesn't add to the cost).
No. of bags:
Gravel: 750 ÷ 50 = 15 bags.
Sand: 375 ÷ 40 = 9.375 = 10 bags.
Cement: 250 ÷ 25 = 10 bags.
Cost of materials = (15 × £4.80) + (10 × £4.10) + (10 × £3.90) = £152.
No delivery charge as total is over £150.
Cheapest way to hire mixer is to use weekend rate plus one additional day = £21.50 + £10.50 = £32.
Total cost = £152 + £32 = £184.

Safety and Design
Page 37
Q1 a) Height of box = 400 mm.
Length = 1400 mm − (2 × 400 mm) = 600 mm.
Width = 1300 mm − (2 × 400 mm) = 500 mm.
b) Volume of a cuboid
= length × width × height
= 600 mm × 500 mm × 400 mm
= 120 000 000 mm³
= 120 000 cm³
= 0.12 m³.

Answers (Higher Level): P.38 — P.41

c) Across the length of the box, there will be space for 600 mm ÷ 150 mm = 4 books. Across the width there will be space for 500 mm ÷ 15 mm = 33 books.
The books can be stacked 400 mm ÷ 200 mm = 2 books high. So the biggest number of books per box = 4 × 33 × 2 = 264.

Q2 If each box is at the upper bound of the weight measurement (i.e. 0.5 kg above the given weight), then the total weight of the boxes will be: (5 × 14.5 kg) + (40 × 3.5 kg) + (10 × 25.5 kg) + (10 × 12.5 kg) + (3 × 74.5 kg) + (9 × 62.5 kg) + (8 × 79.5 kg) = 2014.5 kg. So no, it is not safe for Kim to load all the boxes onto his van.

Page 38

Q3 a) Using Pythagoras' Theorem, if the length of each diagonal bamboo pole is L, then:
$L^2 = 205^2 + 310^2$
$L^2 = 42\,025 + 96\,100 = 138\,125$
$L = \sqrt{138\,125} = 371.6517...$
$L = 372$ cm, to the nearest cm.

b) The lengths of bamboo Constantina needs are:
2 × 310 cm, cut from 3.5 m poles.
2 × 205 cm, cut from 2.5 m poles.
2 × 372 cm, cut from 4.0 m poles.
Lowest total cost = (2 × £4.30) + (2 × £2.90) + (2 × £5.00) = £24.40.

Q4 a) If the height of the wall is h, then:
Tan 75° = $\frac{h}{5}$
$h = 5 \times \tan 75° = 18.6602...$
= 18.7 m to the nearest 10 cm.

b) For each piece of cloth:
Height = 18.7 m ÷ 10 = 1.87 m.
Width = 40.3 m ÷ 10 = 4.03 m.
Area = 1.87 × 4.03 = 7.5361
= 7.5 m² to 1 d.p.

Page 39

Q5 a) Maximum height = 190.5 mm.
Maximum width = 135.5 mm.
Maximum thickness = 14.5 mm.

b) To fit in 100 DVDs as planned, the unit needs to be 50 maximum DVD thicknesses high, plus 49 maximum divider thicknesses, plus 2 maximum wooden shell thicknesses, so:
Height = (50 × 14.5 mm) + (49 × 2.5 mm) + (2 × 17.5 mm)
= 882.5 mm.
The width of the unit is 2 of the maximum DVD heights, plus the width of the dividing panel and 2 of the outer shell thicknesses, so:
Width = (2 × 190.5 mm) + 15.5 mm + (2 × 17.5 mm)
= 431.5 mm.
The depth of the unit is just the maximum width of a DVD
= 135.5 mm.

Q6 a) Tan 5° = $\frac{215}{L}$
$L = \frac{215}{\tan 5°}$ = 2457.4612... mm
= 246 cm to the nearest cm.
Sin 5° = $\frac{215}{R}$
$R = \frac{215}{\sin 5°}$ = 2466.8483... mm
= 247 cm to the nearest cm.

b) Planks are 2.5 m (250 cm) to the nearest 10 cm, so minimum plank length = 250 cm − 5 cm = 245 cm. The ramp uses planks of at least 247 cm, so no, Sam can't be sure that the planks will be long enough.

Page 40

Q7 a) Using Pythagoras' Theorem, if the length of slope is L, then:
$L^2 = 45^2 + (68 - 49)^2$
$L^2 = 45^2 + 19^2 = 2025 + 361 = 2386$
$L = \sqrt{2386} = 48.8466...$ m.
Area of solar panels = 48.8466... m × 22 m = 1075 m², to the nearest m².

b) Angle between slope and horizontal = a.
Tan $a°$ = $\frac{19}{45}$ = 0.4222...
$a°$ = $\tan^{-1} 0.42222$ = 22.8905...
= 23° to the nearest degree.

Q8 Labelling the net with the actual dimensions gives the following:

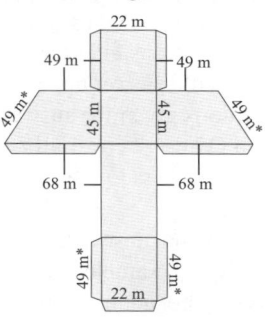

*calculated using Pythagoras' Theorem as in Q7, and rounded to the nearest m.

This gives a total length of the net of: 49 m + 45 m + 68 m + 49 m = 211 m = 211 000 mm.
Total width of the net = 68 m + 22 m + 68 m = 158 m = 158 000 mm.
Using a scale of 1 : 800, the total length of the model net = (211 000 mm ÷ 800) + 5 mm for flap = 268.75 mm = 269 mm to the nearest mm.
The total width of the model net = 158 000 ÷ 800 = 197.5 mm = 198 mm to the nearest mm.
The A4 card is 297 mm long and 210 mm wide, so it is both long enough and wide enough for the net to fit, so Li can use this scale.

Environmental Issues
Page 41

Q1 a) Total of lengths = 66.7 cm
66.7 ÷ 14 = 4.76 cm.

b) 7.1 − 2.4 = 4.7 cm.

Q2 a) The tank holds 2000 litres and there's 1/8 of a tank left.
1/8 × 2000 = 250 litres.

b) 2000 litres cost £1096 so it costs 1096 ÷ 2000 = £0.548 per litre. Melissa paid £465 for oil in March so received 465 ÷ 0.548 = 849 litres (to the nearest litre).

c) Melissa has had 2000 + 849 = 2849 litres of oil delivered since September. She has 250 litres left so has used 2849 − 250 = 2599 litres between September 2009 and September 2010. So she uses an average of 2599 ÷ 12 = 216.6 litres per month.

Answers (Higher Level): P.42 — P.44

Page 42

Q3 a) E.g. Q3 is ambiguous, one person could answer yes, whilst another person who drops litter the same amount could answer no.
The options given for answering Q4 and Q5 don't cover all possible answers to the questions.
People may not answer Q4 truthfully, for example, many pupils may not admit to dropping litter to try to look cool.

b) E.g. How many times a week do you drop litter? Options for answers: 0, 1-5 times, 5-10 times, more than 10 times.

c) E.g. the questionnaire could be distributed during form time as all pupils should be present and it would reach pupils of all ages.

Q4 A suitable chart for showing the amounts of the different types of litter as proportions of the total amount is a pie chart.
Start by adding up the total number of each type of litter found in the school grounds:
Food Wrappers:
17 + 13 + 6 + 11 = 47
Bottles: 8 + 5 + 7 + 3 = 23
Cans: 3 + 1 + 2 + 6 = 12
Other: 10 + 7 + 6 + 7 = 30
Total: 47 + 23 + 12 + 30 = 112.
In the pie chart 360° represents 112 pieces of litter so 360 ÷ 112 = 3.214...° represents 1 piece of litter.
Multiply the number of pieces of litter of each type by 3.214...°:
Food Wrappers: 47 × 3.214... = 151°
Bottles: 23 × 3.214... = 74°
Cans: 12 × 3.214... = 39°
Other: 30 × 3.214... = 96°
Draw and label a pie chart showing these angles:

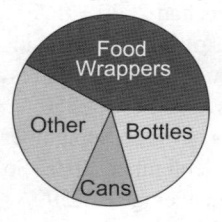

Page 43

Q5 a) Recycled waste:

Mass (kg)	Freq.	Mid-interval	Freq. × Mid-interval
0 ≤ m < 3	29	1.5	43.5
3 ≤ m < 6	34	4.5	153
6 ≤ m < 9	36	7.5	270
9 ≤ m < 12	31	10.5	325.5
12 ≤ m < 15	18	13.5	243

Overall total = 43.5 + 153 + 270 + 325.5 + 243 = 1035 kg.
Frequency total = 29 + 34 + 36 + 31 + 18 = 148 households.
Mean = 1035 ÷ 148 = 7.0 kg.

Landfill waste:

Mass (kg)	Freq.	Mid-interval	Freq. × Mid-interval
0 ≤ m < 5	9	2.5	22.5
5 ≤ m < 10	17	7.5	127.5
10 ≤ m < 15	36	12.5	450
15 ≤ m < 20	52	17.5	910
20 ≤ m < 25	34	22.5	765

Overall total = 22.5 + 127.5 + 450 + 910 + 765 = 2275 kg.
Frequency total = 9 + 17 + 36 + 52 + 34 = 148 households.
Mean = 2275 ÷ 148 = 15.4 kg.
The mean amount of waste sent to landfill by each household is more than twice as much as the mean amount of waste they recycle.

b) The total amount of rubbish recycled each week = 1035 kg.
Total amount of rubbish = 1035 kg + 2275 kg = 3310 kg.
So the percentage that is recycled = 1035 kg ÷ 3310 kg × 100% = 31.3%.

Q6 Carl has driven 59975 − 59817 = 158 miles. He has used the same amount of petrol that he put in the tank at Gulfaco, as he started with a full tank. He spent £21.66 on petrol so used 21.66 ÷ 1.14 = 19 litres. From conversion chart, 19 litres = 4.2 gallons. Carl's car did 158 miles on 4.2 gallons, which is 158 ÷ 4.2 = 37.6 miles per gallon.

Health and Fitness

Page 44

Q1 a) For mean scores, add up the scores for each person and divide by 5:
Asif: 28.4   Brad: 25.8
Christian: 34.4   Declan: 36.6
Ezra: 33.6   Fintan: 29.6
George: 23.8   Hermez: 30.6
So Declan is the winner as he has the highest mean score.

b) For mean scores, add up the scores for each activity and divide by 8:
Press-ups: 24.5   Sit-ups: 38.5
Chin-ups: 16.0   Dips: 23.9
Squats: 48.9
So time on 'squats' should be reduced.

c) The least consistent activity has the highest range of scores:
Press-ups: 34 − 12 = 22
Sit-ups: 56 − 24 = 32
Chin-ups: 22 − 8 = 14
Dips: 35 − 18 = 17
Squats: 61 − 37 = 24
So 'sit-ups' should be changed.

Q2 a) E.g.:
Members wouldn't go to the class if they didn't like it, so Q1 is not very useful;
Q2 assumes that they dislike one activity whereas they may like all of them, or dislike many;
Q3 is a leading question so the members may feel forced to agree with Anna about the skipping.

Answers (Higher Level): P.45 — P.47

b) E.g.:
Q1. Do you feel the circuit training class would be improved by changing one or more of the activities? (Yes / No).
Q2. Which activity do you enjoy the least? (Press-ups / Sit-ups / Chin-ups / Dips / Squats)
Q3. Which of the following activities would you prefer to be included in the classes? (Skipping plus a few other options).

Page 45

Q3 a) Marcus' mean calorie intake for the week is (1700 + 1850 + 2000 + 1800 + 1850 + 2400 + 1700) ÷ 7 = 13 300 ÷ 7 = 1900, so Marcus did not meet his target.

b) Marcus' normal calorie intake should be 2500 × 7 = 17 500 per week. For the week shown he has had 17 500 − 13 300 = 4200 calories under what he needs to maintain his weight, so he should lose 4200 ÷ 3500 = 1.2 lbs per week.

Q4 a) Dominic has to do the following:
0.5 km swim in 10 mins at an average speed of
0.5 km ÷ (10 mins ÷ 60) = 3 km/h; 5 mins to change;
7.5 km cycle in 25 mins at an average speed of
7.5 km ÷ (25 mins ÷ 60) = 18 km/h; 2.5 mins to change;
2 km run in 17.5 mins at an average speed of 2 km ÷ (17.5 mins ÷ 60) = 6.86 km/h (to 3 s.f.).

b) Target time for whole session is 60 mins, so he needs to finish the run by 11.15. If he gets off the bike at 11.03 and changes in 2 mins, he will have 10 mins left to complete the run.

c) Dominic can swim 0.5 km in 10 mins, so the 1 km swim should take him 20 mins.
He can cycle 7.5 km in 25 mins so the 20 km cycle should take him (20 km ÷ 7.5 km) × 25 mins = 67 mins (to the nearest minute).
He can run 2 km in 17.5 mins, so a 5 km run should take him (5 km ÷ 2 km) × 17.5 mins = 44 mins (to the nearest minute).
Total time = 20 + 67 + 44 + 5 + 2.5 = 138.5 minutes (or 2 h 19 mins, to the nearest minute).

Page 46

Q5 a) G, as they are shorter and heavier than the trend.

b) BMI = 96 kg ÷ (1.53 m)² = 41.0. So person G is classed as obese by BMI.

c) E.g. D seems taller and lighter than the class trend. BMI = 75 kg ÷ (1.84 m)² = 22.2. This is in the 'healthy' range, so it's unlikely they need to lose weight.

Q6 a) Cassie's graph shows negative correlation between BMI and class attendance, i.e. the more classes you attend, the lower your BMI.

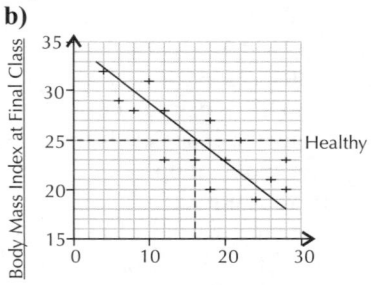

b)

From line of best fit, minimum number of classes to be within 'healthy' range ≈ 16.

Page 47

Q7 Start Weights:

Midpoint (x)	Frequency (f)	x × f
85	4	340
95	7	665
105	11	1155
115	5	575
125	3	375

Mean Start Weight =
Overall Total ÷ Frequency Total =
3110 ÷ 30 = 103.67 kg.

End Weights:

Midpoint (x)	Frequency (f)	x × f
75	2	150
85	11	935
95	8	760
105	5	525
115	4	460

Mean End Weight =
Overall Total ÷ Frequency Total =
2830 ÷ 30 = 94.33 kg.
Difference in weights =
103.67 kg − 94.33 kg =
9.3 kg (1 d.p.).
So Cassie could say in the press release that previous members have lost over 9 kg on average.

Q8

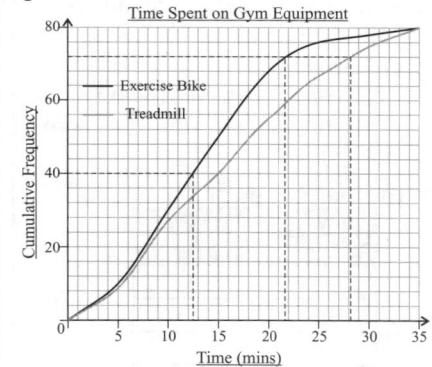

a) From cumulative frequency curves shown above, the median times are:
Exercise Bike: 12.5 mins
Treadmill: 15 mins.

Answers (Higher Level): P.48 — P.50

b) To find top 10%, draw a line at a CF of 80 − 8 = 72, as shown above. Top 10% of bike users stay on for around 22 mins and above so 22 mins could be the limit for the bike. Top 10% of treadmill users stay on for around 28 mins and above, so 28 mins could be the limit for the treadmill.

Running a Business
Page 48
Q1 a) Sales for June =
£20 000 − 20% of £20 000 =
£20 000 − (20 ÷ 100 × £20 000)
= £16 000.
E.g. Bar chart / bar line graph:

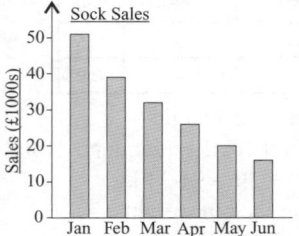

b) E.g. The sales are decreasing each month / the sales decrease by a smaller amount each month / the sales decrease by around 20% each month / they have decreased by around 70% in six months etc.

c) Sales for July =
£16 000 − 20% of £16 000 =
£16 000 − (20 ÷ 100 × £16 000)
= £12 800.

Q2 a) From Sy's graph:

Pairs of Socks Sold Daily	Frequency
0 – 9	13
10 – 19	25
20 – 29	35
30 – 39	47
40 – 49	42
50 – 59	18

Modal group is the group with the highest frequency, so for Suki's shop it's 10-19 socks, and for Sy's it's 30-39 socks.
Total frequency = 18 + 76 + 52 + 22 + 12 = 180 days, so median is at (180 + 1) ÷ 2 = 90.5th position. In Suki's shop this lies in the 10-19 socks group, and in Sy's it lies in the 30-39 socks group.

b) Sy's shop should have the highest total sales because each day he sells more pairs of socks on average.

c) The biggest possible range in daily sock sales in Suki's shop is 49 − 0 = 49, whereas in Sy's shop it is 59 − 0 = 59. Since Suki has the smaller range in sock sales, she has the most consistency.

Page 49
Q3 a) From the graph, to make £400 Glenn will need to sell around 1150 bars. At 200 bars per week, this will take him 1150 ÷ 200 = 5.75 weeks = 6 full weeks.

b) From the graph, Glenn expects to make £700 for every 2000 bars sold, which means a selling price of £700 ÷ 2000 = £0.35 per bar.
In one year (52 weeks), he should sell 52 × 200 = 10 400 bars, so total revenue = 10 400 × £0.35 = £3640.

Q4 a) The probabilities of people in each age group buying the chocolate can be estimated using relative frequencies as follows:
0-19: 3 ÷ 11 = 0.2727
20-39: 15 ÷ 23 = 0.6522
40-59: 22 ÷ 46 = 0.4783
60-79: 4 ÷ 12 = 0.3333
80+: 3 ÷ 8 = 0.375.
So the age group most likely to buy the chocolate is the 20-39 year old group.

b) Probability of a 20-39 year old buying the chocolate = 0.6522, so of the 350 people in the sample, Glenn should expect 0.6522 × 350 = 228 people to buy chocolate.

Page 50
Q5 a) Q1 sales: £70 000 + £80 500 + £92 600 = £243 100.
Q2 sales: £106 500 + £122 500 + £140 900 = £369 900.
% Increase =
(£369 900 − £243 100) ÷ £243 100 × 100% =
52.1596...% increase.
If this increase continues in Q3, then total sales will be £369 900 + 52.2%.
52.2 ÷ 100 × £369 900 = £192 938.38.
So Q3 sales should be:
£369 900 + £192 938.38 = £562 800, to the nearest £100.

b) % of total sales from Amir's shop:
Q1: (£49 000 + £56 400 + £64 800) ÷ £243 100 × 100% = 70.0%.
Q2: (£74 600 + £85 800 + £98 600) ÷ £369 900 × 100% = 70.0%.
So if Amir's shop accounts for 70% of the total sales, then he should make 70 ÷ 100 × £562 800 = £394 000 in Q3, to the nearest £100.

Q6 a) From the graph, 950 000 trucks have been made in the last 50 days, so average rate = 950 000 ÷ 50 = 19 000 trucks per day.

b) The highest rate is where the graph is steepest, i.e. between days 25-35.
During these weeks the rate was (800 000 − 500 000) ÷ 10 = 30 000 trucks per day. This means the order of 550 000 would be done in 550 000 ÷ 30 000 = 18.3333... = 19 days.

Answers (Higher Level): P.51 — P.54

Page 51

Q7 Of 1500 leaflets delivered:
9 ÷ 10 × 1500 = 1350 will go to potential new customers,
8 ÷ 100 × 1350 = 108 will get in touch, 7 ÷ 9 × 108 = 84 will become new customers. Dhruv should make in total 84 × £235 = £19 740 per year from these customers. From the graph, 1500 leaflets will cost 7.5p per leaflet to print, so total cost of leaflets = 1500 × £0.075 = £112.50, so Dhruv's extra income will be £19 740 − £112.50 = £19 627.50.

Q8 Total taxable income =
(135 × 48 × £6.40)
+ (20 ÷ 100 × £6.40 × 135)
− (£65 × 48) − £300
= £41 472 + £172.80 − £3120 − £300 = £38 224.80.
(£37 400 − £6475) = £30 925 will be taxed at 20% and
(£38 224.80 − £37 400) = £824.80 will be taxed at 40%.
Total tax to be paid =
(20 ÷ 100 × £30 925)
+ (40 ÷ 100 × £824.80) =
£6185 + £329.92 = £6514.92.
This will leave Dhruv with
£38 224.80 − £6514.92 =
£31 709.88.

Hospitals and Healthcare
Page 52

Q1 a) Number of patients =
84% of 1300 = 0.84 × 1300 = 1092.
Number of vegetarians = 9% of 1092 = 0.09 × 1092 = 98 (to nearest whole number).
Number of vegetarian meals per day = 98 × 2 = 196.
So Julian needs at least 196.

b) Number of patients needing low fat meals = 17% of 1092 = 0.17 × 1092 = 186 (to nearest whole number).
Number of low fat meals per day = 186 × 2 = 372.
So Julian needs at least 372.

c) The probability that a patient is a vegetarian AND on a low fat diet = P(veg) × P(low fat) = 0.09 × 0.17 = 0.0153.
On a typical day there are 1092 patients, so there will be:
0.0153 × 1092 = 17 vegetarians on a low fat diet.

Q2 a) Estimated probability = no. people on low fat diet ÷ no. of people sampled. Over the whole week there were a total of 120 people on low fat diets and 700 sampled, so probability = 120 ÷ 700 = 0.171 or 17.1 % to 3 s.f.

b) The more people in Julian's sample, the better the estimate for the probability; so he could collect data for longer than one week or have more than 100 people in his sample each day.

Page 53

Q3 a)

No. of new infections in one week (x)	No. of weeks (f)	x × f
0	1	0
1	2	2
2	7	14
3	5	15
4	3	12
5	2	10

Since the introduction of the handwash, Mean = overall total ÷ frequency total = 53 ÷ 20 = 2.65 infections per week.
If the handwash reduced infections by 50% there would only be 2 per week, so the handwash is not as effective as the makers claim.

b) Probability = 2.65 infections per week ÷ 16 patients = 0.166, or 16.6% to 3 s.f.

Q4 a) The only way two non-sufferers could have a baby that suffers from the disease is if both were carriers.
P(carrier) = $\frac{1}{30}$, so: P(both) = P(carrier) × P(carrier) = $\frac{1}{30} \times \frac{1}{30} = \frac{1}{900}$.
In this case, the chance of their baby being a sufferer is 25% or $\frac{1}{4}$ so: P(baby sufferer) = $\frac{1}{900} \times \frac{1}{4} = \frac{1}{3600}$.

b) P(carrier) has been reduced to $\frac{1}{300}$ so P(baby sufferer) = $\frac{1}{300} \times \frac{1}{300} \times \frac{1}{4} = \frac{1}{360\,000}$.

Page 54

Q5 a) Total number of patients each year = 4000 (from graph), and 98% of these must be seen in 18 weeks or less. 98% of 4000 = 0.98 × 4000 = 3920.

b) Year 1 target would be 0.9 × 4000 = 3600 patients within 18 weeks.
Year 2 target would be 0.95 × 4000 = 3800 patients within 18 weeks.

From graph, in Year 1 they only saw 3400 patients, so were under target. In Year 2 they saw 3800 so were on target.

Answers (Higher Level): P.55 — P.58

Q6

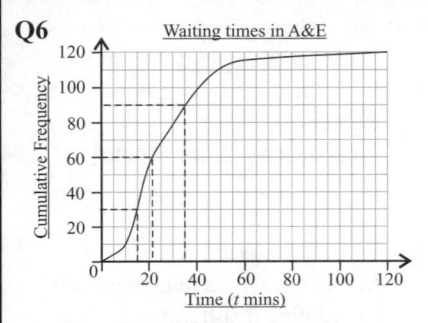

Waiting times in A&E (cumulative frequency graph)

From a cumulative frequency graph:
Median = 21 mins, so they are not meeting their target for a 20 min average wait time.
'Middle 50%' is equivalent to the Interquartile range.
Upper quartile = 35 mins
Lower quartile = 15 mins
Interquartile range = 35 − 15 = 20 mins, so they are meeting their target for a 20 minute interquartile range.

Local Council Issues
Page 55
Q1 a) Total no. of residents = 10 950.
  i) (962 + 831) ÷ 10 950 × 100% = 16.4%
  ii) (4073 + 1167) ÷ 10 950 × 100% = 47.9%
  iii) 622 ÷ 10 950 × 100% = 5.7%
b) Median position = 10 951 ÷ 2 = 5475.5th place. This lies in the age group 25-44.
c) She should recommend the centre for evening classes. The modal group is the 25-44 age group, and the median age is also in this group. This age group is most likely to be working and take advantage of the evening classes.

Q2 a) 1) How old are you? (with at least 3 option boxes with appropriate age ranges for each, with no gaps or overlaps, and first and last boxes to have 'xxx and under' and 'xxx and over' so all ages are covered).

2) How often do you visit the library per month / year? (with at least 3 option boxes with appropriate numerical ranges, with no gaps or overlaps and all possible answers covered).
b) Kay should take a stratified sample of the town residents which has the same proportion of the different age ranges as the whole town.
c) E.g. Kay could telephone people or question them in person so she has their response straight away / she could offer an incentive such as a prize draw for people to return postal questionnaires / she could make sure that questionnaires sent by post include a postage paid envelope for replies.

Page 56
Q3 a) 2009 mean = 60 ÷ 12 = 5 accidents per month.
2010 mean = 66 ÷ 12 = 5.5 accidents per month.
So Trevor is correct — the mean number of accidents per month has increased.
b) In 2009 the mode and the median number of accidents were both 6, and in 2010 the mode was 3 and median was 4, so the council could use the mode to justify their claim.

Q4 a) Total angle size for 'In favour' and 'Strongly in favour' = 126° + 18° = 144°. Percentage = 144° ÷ 360° × 100% = 40%.
b) If only 40% of residents are in favour of having the cameras removed, then 60% do not want them removed. There is also a higher proportion strongly against having them removed than are strongly in favour of removing them.

Page 57
Q5 a) See below. Check scale is 2 cm : 1 km and construction marks have been left in place.

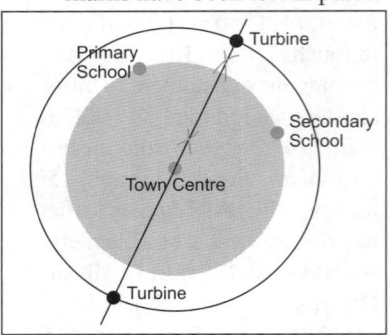

b)

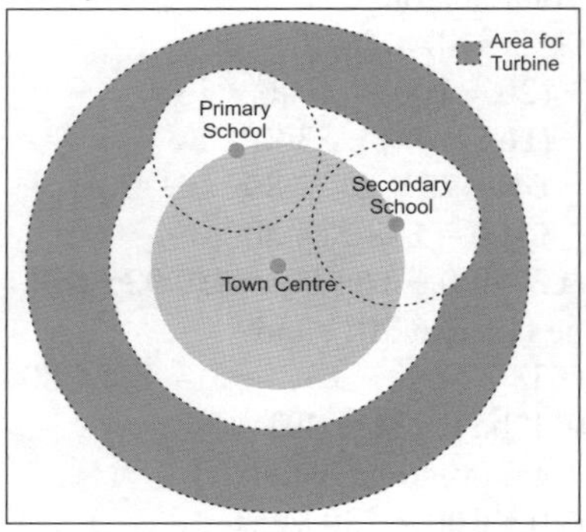

Q6 Total no. of members = 250.
Males to invite:
16-24: 21 ÷ 250 × 20 = 2
25-44: 30 ÷ 250 × 20 = 2
45-64: 47 ÷ 250 × 20 = 4
65+: 24 ÷ 250 × 20 = 2
Females to invite:
16-24: 12 ÷ 250 × 20 = 1
25-44: 41 ÷ 250 × 20 = 3
45-64: 31 ÷ 250 × 20 = 2
65+: 44 ÷ 250 × 20 = 4

Page 58
Q7 a) Total amount of money available in 2010 was:
£1200 × 500 000 = £600 000 000 = £600 million.
Of this, the Police Authority had: (54° ÷ 360° × £600M) = £90M.
For 2011, the Police Authority will need an extra 3% of £90 = 0.03 × £90M = £2.7M.
So in total the council will need: £600M + £2.7M = £602.7M in 2011. This is an increase of £2.7M ÷ £600M × 100% = 0.45%.

Answers (Higher Level): P.59 — P.61

b) If all bills rise by 0.45%, this will be an increase in the average bill of: 0.0045 × £1200 = £5.40, which is £5 to the nearest pound, so Seb is right.

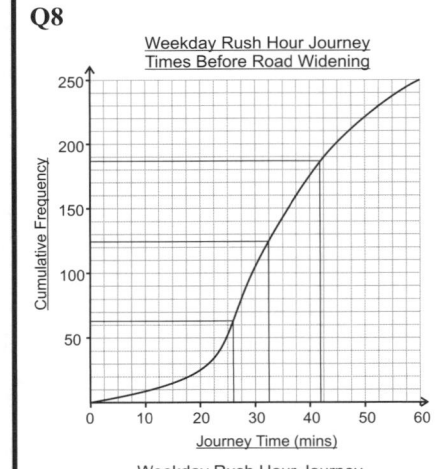

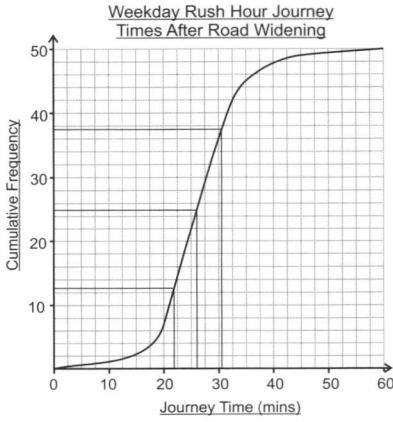

Q8

Weekday Rush Hour Journey Times Before Road Widening

Weekday Rush Hour Journey Times After Road Widening

Median before ≈ 32.5 mins
Median after ≈ 26.5 mins
Looking at the IQR:
IQR before ≈ 42 − 26 = 16 mins
IQR after ≈ 31 − 22 = 9 mins
The council are right in claiming that the spending was justified, because the average journey time has decreased by around 6 mins, and the interquartile range has reduced too, so journey times are now more consistent.

Science in the Workplace
Page 59
Q1 a) 0.000004 m = 4×10^{-6} m.
1×10^{-6} m = 1 μm,
so 4×10^{-6} m = 4 μm.
b) Samples should be 5 cells thick.
5×4 μm = 20 μm, so yes, the sample is the correct thickness.
c) 0.0000015 m = 1.5×10^{-6} m.
1×10^{-6} m = 1 μm,
so 1.5×10^{-6} m = 1.5 μm.
Maximum detector reading = 5×1.5 μm = 7.5 μm.

Q2 a) Soraya has 5 hours between 8 am and 1 pm. The sample of 1×10^{10} will double (× 2) every hour, so after 5 hours there will be: $(1 \times 10^{10}) \times 2^5 = 3.2 \times 10^{11}$. This is smaller than the amount she needs (1×10^{12}) so no, she will not have a large enough sample by 1 pm.
b) $1 \times 10^{12} \div 10 = 10^{12} \div 10^1 = 10^{(12-1)} = 10^{11}$ (or 1×10^{11}) in each sample.

Page 60
Q3 a) Each sheet is a cuboid with volume = 210 mm × 297 mm × 0.15 mm.
In metres, 1000 mm = 1 m, so Volume = 0.21 m × 0.297 m × 0.00015 m = 9.355×10^{-6} m^3.
There are 500 sheets in one packet, and the order is for 60 packets, so total volume = 9.355×10^{-6} m^3 × 500 × 60 = 0.281 m^3, to 3 s.f.
b) Mass of pulp required = 0.281 m^3 × 667 kg = 187.427 kg.
80% of 187.427 kg = 80 ÷ 100 × 187.427 = 149.9416 kg = 150 kg to nearest kg.

Q4 a) If the grammage (G) is directly proportional to the thickness (T), then:
$G = kT$, where k is a constant.
For the print grade paper,
80 = k × 0.12
k = $\frac{80}{0.12}$ = $666\frac{2}{3}$.
Check this is the same for art grade paper:
100 = k × 0.15
k = $\frac{100}{0.15}$ = $666\frac{2}{3}$.
So Arthur could use the formula:
$G = 666\frac{2}{3}T$.
b) Using the formula,
$G = 666\frac{2}{3} \times 0.18 = 120$ g/m^2.
c) From the values given and calculated:

T (mm)	0.12	0.15	0.18
G (g/m^2)	80	100	120

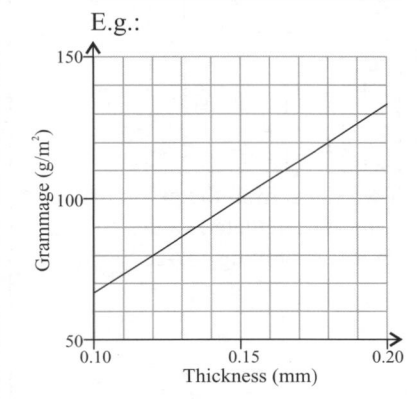

E.g.:

Page 61
Q5 a) From the graph, at 0.1 mm, detector reading = 24%.
b) 10% of 0.1 mm = (10 ÷ 100) × 0.1 mm = 0.01 mm.
So the warning light should come on when the thickness is 0.1 + 0.01 = 0.11 mm, and 0.1 − 0.01 = 0.09 mm. From the graph, the detector readings at these thicknesses are 22% and 30%.

Answers (Higher Level): P.62

Q6 a) Detector reading (D) is inversely proportional to thickness (T), so:
$T = \frac{k}{D}$. When $T = 0.1$, $D = 30$, so:
$0.1 = \frac{k}{30}$
$k = 30 \times 0.1 = 3$, so the equation is:
$T = \frac{3}{D}$.

b) Rearranging the equation gives $D = \frac{3}{T}$. When $T = 0.5$, $D = \frac{3}{0.5} = 6\%$, so the alarm should go off when the detector reads 6%.

Page 62

Q7 E.g.

Speed (mph)	Actual Braking Distance from Graph (metres)	Correct Braking Distance using $B = 0.015S^2$ (metres).
10	1.5	1.5
20	6	6
30	13.5	13.5

The values from the graph match with the calculated values so yes, the car is braking correctly.

Q8

S (mph)	T (metres)	B (metres)	Overall Stopping Distance (metres)
0	0	0	0
10	3	1.5	4.5
20	6	6	12
30	9	13.5	22.5
40	12	24	36
50	15	37.5	52.5
60	18	54	72
70	21	73.5	94.5

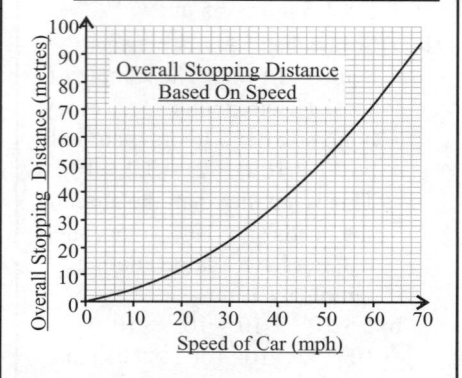

Overall Stopping Distance Based On Speed